Beyond Wanting

Beyond Wanting

The Art of True Manifestation

• • • • •

MATT COOKE

TARCHER
an imprint of Penguin Random House
New York

Tarcher

an imprint of Penguin Random House LLC
1745 Broadway, New York, NY 10019
penguinrandomhouse.com

Most Tarcher books are available at a discount when purchased in quantity for sales promotions or corporate use. Special editions, which include personalized covers, excerpts, and corporate imprints, can be created when purchased in large quantities. For more information, please e-mail specialmarkets@penguinrandomhouse.com. Your local bookstore can also assist with discounted bulk purchases using the Penguin Random House corporate Business-to-Business program. For assistance in locating a participating retailer, e-mail B2B@penguinrandomhouse.com.

Book design by Daniel Brount

Library of Congress Cataloging-in-Publication Data
has been applied for.
ISBN 9780593853306 (hardcover)
ISBN 9780593853313 (ebook)

Printed in the United States of America
1st Printing

The authorized representative in the EU for product safety and compliance is Penguin Random House Ireland, Morrison Chambers, 32 Nassau Street, Dublin D02 YH68, Ireland, https://eu-contact.penguin.ie.

For my wife, Corisande—
you are my everything

Contents

CONTENTS

INTRODUCTION

Have you ever felt the intense ache of wanting something so badly, yet it always seems just out of reach? Perhaps it's financial freedom, a relationship, or that dream job you've been eyeing. You've tried visualizing, affirming, and maybe even creating vision boards, but your desire remains frustratingly elusive. What if I told you that this very wanting—this desperate longing—is precisely what's keeping your dreams at arm's length?

Welcome to the paradox at the heart of manifestation: You don't attract what you want. You attract what you are.

Let that sink in for a moment. It's a concept so deceptively simple yet profoundly transformative that it has the power to revolutionize how you approach manifestation—and how you live your entire life.

This book is your wake-up call. It's time to move beyond wanting and step into being.

Think about it: Why did you pick up this book? What drove you to these pages? Was it a gnawing dissatisfaction with your current circumstances? A burning desire for change? Or a curiosity about the true nature of reality and your place within it?

Whatever your reason, you're in the right place. Because here's the truth that most manifestation teachings miss: you are always in a state of manifestation, whether you're conscious of it or not. Every moment of every day, you're broadcasting a signal to the Universe—a vibrational frequency as unique as your fingerprint. And the Universe, in its infinite wisdom, is constantly responding, mirroring to you the exact essence of that signal.

The challenge most of us face isn't with manifestation itself; it's with how we approach it. This is a crucial distinction that changes everything. We've been unconsciously manifesting all along, like radio towers broadcasting on autopilot, unaware of the program we're transmitting. Each thought, each feeling, each belief acts as a signal we're constantly sending out. The irony is that our unconscious broadcast is often steeped in wanting, in lacking, in the very absence of what we desire. We unknowingly transmit frequencies of scarcity, doubt, and separation—the exact opposite of what we're trying to manifest. But what if you could change the station? What if you could consciously choose your broadcasting frequency, aligning it precisely with the reality you wish to create?

This book will show you how. Drawing on cutting-edge science, ancient wisdom, and real-world success stories, we'll explore the quantum field of infinite possibilities surrounding us. You'll discover how your thoughts, emotions, and beliefs shape this field, collapsing waves of potential into the particles of your experienced reality.

I know what you're thinking. "Science? In a book about manifestation?" I get it. I was once the ultimate skeptic. If someone had told me a few years ago that we could turn our thoughts into physical reality, I would have laughed them out of the room. But when we dig deep, a surprising amount of scientific research supports the principles of manifestation.

As a former skeptic, I invite you to approach this book with an open mind. Some concepts might challenge your current beliefs, but I encourage you to suspend judgment. Give yourself permission to fully explore these ideas. Test the techniques for yourself. You might be surprised by what you discover. Throughout this book, I've grounded concepts of manifestation in scientific research wherever possible. You'll find references to quantum physics, neuroscience, and psychology that support these principles. However, I also acknowledge that there's still much to be understood about the nature of consciousness and reality. Remember, skepticism can be valuable when balanced with openness to new ideas. As you read, feel free to question, ponder, and critically examine the concepts presented. But also allow yourself to experience the practices firsthand. Your own experiences will ultimately be your most convincing evidence.

This book isn't just theory. You'll also find practical, applicable wisdom that you can start using today. You'll learn how to do the following:

- Identify and reprogram the subconscious patterns that are sabotaging your manifestations

- Harness the power of your thoughts and emotions to amplify your creative force
- Use meditation, journaling, gratitude, and affirmations to realign your energy
- Recognize and interpret the signs and synchronicities guiding you toward your desires
- Take aligned, inspired action that resonates with your new vibrational state

When you finish this book, you won't just understand manifestation—you'll live it. You'll have the tools to transcend mere wanting and step into a state of being that naturally attracts your desires. This isn't about forcing outcomes or manipulating reality. It's about aligning yourself so perfectly with your desires that they can't help but materialize in your life. It's about becoming the person who already has what they seek rather than the person who's desperately chasing after it.

Why I Wrote This Book

I'm going to be honest with you. I wrote this book for my younger self. It's the book I wish existed in some of my hardest moments. This book culminates an extraordinary journey from a skeptical, suit-and-tie-wearing corporate professional to a globally recognized manifestation coach. As you will read in chapter 1, my story begins with a profound spiritual awakening that shook me to my core. It shattered my understanding of reality and forced me to see the world through a new lens. This awakening set me on a path to discovering the hidden truths of our reality—truths that go far beyond what meets the eye.

I'm not special. I struggled in school, always feeling a step behind my peers. I didn't graduate with a fancy degree or have any apparent advantages. Like many of you, I'm just a regular person who has always dreamed of living the best life possible. And I began my journey with complete disbelief. I wasn't seeking spiritual enlightenment or manifestation techniques. I was a hard-nosed corporate guy who believed in only what I could see and touch. I understand the doubts, questions, and resistance many feel when first encountering these concepts.

I've been there and found a way to bridge the gap between the mystical, practical, spiritual, and scientific. Writing this book has always been a dream of mine, and the fact that you're reading it now proves the power of the principles I'm about to teach you. This book is a manifestation in action. I've woven my personal story—my struggles, breakthroughs, and ups and downs—throughout these pages to illustrate how manifestation principles work in a real-life context.

You'll witness how I manifested some of my biggest dreams using the exact methods I share with you. But this isn't just about me. You'll read about my clients who have manifested extraordinary outcomes, too. I've also drawn upon a century's worth of research from brilliant scientists who have walked this path before me. Although you can't simply google "the science of manifestation," that doesn't mean it isn't real. We can all relate to those strange coincidences, those moments of perfect timing that seem too good to be true. In this book, I'll show you that these aren't just random occurrences, but evidence of the measurable ways our thoughts and beliefs influence our experienced reality.

My goal is simple: to help you understand that you can be anyone, have anything, and create any life you want. If I—a regular person who previously always struggled—can do it, why can't you? This book is for everyone. Whether you're entirely new to the concept of manifestation, vaguely familiar with the law of attraction, or an experienced practitioner looking to refine your skills, you'll find valuable insights and practical techniques here. It's for anyone ready to go beyond wanting—to transform from dreaming about a better life to actually creating it.

How to Read This Book

It might seem presumptuous to tell you how to read a book, but trust me, this is important. Manifestation isn't just a concept; it's a journey. And like any journey, your path matters as much as the destination. This book is designed to transform you from the inside out. Each chapter builds upon the last, guiding you from the foundations of manifestation to advanced techniques and real-world applications. You might be tempted to skip to the chapters that excite you most. I get it. But here's the thing: If you do that, it's like getting a helicopter ride to the top of a mountain without learning how to climb. Sure, you'll reach the summit, but you'll miss out on the most crucial part—the journey that transforms you.

Here's what I'm asking: Read this book sequentially, step-by-step. It's designed this way for a reason. You're not just reading about manifestation; you're also learning to embody the art of manifestation.

Think of each chapter as a level in a game. By chapter 13, you'll have mastered the formula for manifestation. More importantly, you'll find a practice section at the end of each chapter. These carefully crafted exercises are designed to help you implement what you've read. Let's face it: all the knowledge in the world is only helpful if you apply it. This book is a tool, a guide, and a companion on your journey to becoming a conscious creator. It's worth noting that this isn't a quick-fix program promising instant results.

Manifestation is more than a one-and-done deal. It's a skill you develop over time. You might find yourself dwelling in a particular chapter, honing a specific manifestation aspect for a while. That's okay. Take your time. In fact, it's more than okay—it's part of the process. As you work through this book, you're not just learning about manifestation; you're also rewiring your brain, shifting your energy, and aligning with the version of yourself who has already manifested everything you desire. Remember that manifestation is both an art and a science. It requires practice, patience, and persistence. But with the right tools and mindset, you have the power to create extraordinary changes in your life.

In closing, I offer an invitation. You may feel inspired to take immediate action, try a technique, shift a belief, or set a new intention. I wholeheartedly encourage you to do so. Don't wait to finish the book before you start manifesting. Let each page be a catalyst for change in your life. Turn the page, and let's begin. Your new life is waiting.

CHAPTER 1

The Foundations of Manifestation

Everything I knew about life completely changed one evening as I was falling asleep. My wife, Corisande, and I were lying in bed watching Netflix, and as I turned over to go to sleep, out of nowhere, a very strange sensation spread across my body, almost like a vibration. It wasn't painful, so I allowed it to continue. Then, I heard a high-pitched ringing in both of my ears before everything went silent.

Out of nowhere, I heard a voice. Initially it was faint and sounded as if it were coming from the opposite end of a sports hall, gradually getting closer and closer. Then I heard my mother. "Matt, it's Mom. Can you hear me?" Stunned and shocked, I replied, "Yes, Mom, I can hear you." My mind started to spin. I couldn't think straight. I mumbled, "Mom, where are you?" Then, the reality really hit me.

I was speaking to my late mother, Julie, who had passed away almost two years before. As you can imagine, this knocked me for six. "How is this even possible?" I remember thinking. Our brief exchange was interrupted when Corisande gently nudged me, innocently asking, "Matt, who are you talking to?" As I glanced her way, the connection with my mother vanished. She was gone.

Lying in bed, I recall wondering how this had even happened. How will anyone believe me? One moment, I'm living a normal life, juggling a corporate job, with no concept of spirituality, and in a split second, my whole concept of reality is thrown upside down. Imagine having a conversation with a loved one who has passed away. It's not an occasion you can ever prepare for. Let's just say my life has never been the same since.

I became obsessed with the mystical and couldn't get enough of it. Night after night, I lay in bed, hoping to reconnect with my mother, but it never happened again. Somehow, unconsciously, it had happened without my planning, and that's when it clicked. I didn't "want" it to happen; it just did.

When people ask me what the experience was like, I explain that it's like tuning in to an old radio station. Initially, as you search through the channels, there is a strange vibration sound, like static, and then, out of nowhere, you land on one specific frequency and the music comes through loud and clear. That's the best way to describe what happened—an unseen but felt frequency that connected my mom and me, even for a moment. A medium friend of mine has since explained that mediums are called *mediums* because they help people connect in the "middle," which I thought was a brilliant analogy.

I had so many questions, but the answers to what happened were hard to come by. So I did what any person would do: I read every book on the subject and consumed every video that was even somewhat relevant. I watched the film *The Secret*, in which I first heard about energy, vibration, and the Law of Attraction. *The Secret* introduced the foundations of manifestation through a powerful idea: the Universe vibrates with energy, and our thoughts play a pivotal role in shaping our external reality.

Even though my journey started with a connection to the afterlife, I knew that manifestation was my true calling. I was hooked, and my love for mysticism, energy, attraction, and the unseen has been a passion and calling ever since.

The more I learned, the more I noticed changes in my day-to-day life. Every moment not consumed by my full-time job was spent reading, listening, and learning. Each of the following added layers to my understanding: *The Secret* creator Rhonda Byrne's writing became my initial guide. Law of Attraction teacher Bob Proctor's insights into visualization and the Law of Vibration quickly followed. Esther and Jerry Hicks's work channeling the teachings of Abraham (a collective consciousness they connect with) on the Law of Attraction; the timeless wisdom of Napoleon Hill's *Think and Grow Rich*; the philosophical depths of spiritual teacher Eckhart Tolle and the present moment; the spiritual guidance of bestselling author Dr. Wayne Dyer; the ground-breaking work of Dr. Joe Dispenza, who blends neuroscience, epigenetics, and quantum physics; the profound teachings on surrender and consciousness from *The Untethered Soul* author Michael A. Singer; and the teachings of manifestation pioneer Neville Goddard were each essential to my understanding, and I am extremely grateful for them.

Coincidence or Synchronicity?

As I continued to explore these areas of thought and reflect on my life, I became aware of some unusual patterns. Like my connection with my mother, we have all experienced strange, unexplainable phenomena in our lives. Have you ever been thinking of someone, only to have them call or message you out of the blue moments later? Or, have you thought about something, only for it to be said at that exact moment on the TV? Do you constantly notice the repeating patterns of numbers such as 11:11 or 22:22 on the clock, car license plates, time stamps on messages, and packages in the mail? Have you had a dream that then unfolded in real life? Have you heard a song on the radio, read a page in a book, or overheard a stranger's conversation that offered you the exact guidance you needed to move forward in that moment? Or, have you experienced the perfect timing of meeting someone who changed your life forever?

Only when you stop and think about it do you realize that these "coincidences" have been happening your whole life, subtly, in the background, without you even realizing it. Are they coincidences, or is there a hidden force behind the scenes? Could you be connected to an invisible intelligence that's communicating through you? Have you always been tapped into something bigger, a creative force constantly shaping your external reality in every moment of every day?

This book is your wake-up call. My goals are to show you that what you might call coincidences are manifestations of your own creation, and also to shine a light on exactly how you created them. In fact, everything in your life has been created by you, whether you're conscious of it or not. Look at your life now; was your house, wealth, health, relationship, children, or success in your career or business once a dream that existed in your mind?

However, you might be thinking your life is far from a dream. You may be facing challenges, setbacks, or a general sense of dissatisfaction with your current circumstances. If that's the case, I want you to know that you're not alone, and it doesn't mean that manifestation isn't working for you. Once you learn the techniques in this book, you will understand exactly how to consciously manifest what you want and start living your best life.

You are a creator, and you have always been. From the moment you were born, manifestation has been a part of you. It's neither magic nor reserved for the elite; it's your natural state. Every thought you think, emotion you feel, action you take, and belief you hold is constantly shaping your external world. It's time to stop running on autopilot, letting your past, fears, limitations, and disappointments shape your life. This is your moment to take the wheel and steer your life in your desired direction. I'm going to show you exactly how to do that.

But before we discuss the practical steps, let's examine the roots of this powerful concept. Although manifestation has recently become trendy, its principles have been recognized and practiced by people across cultures and traditions for centuries.

A Believer and a Skeptic

In my search for validation, I discovered that manifestation principles had been documented by serious thinkers long before the modern era. One such book was *The Science of Getting Rich* by Wallace D. Wattles, published in 1910. In his work, Wattles emphasized a timeless principle: individuals have the power to shape their reality through their thoughts, focusing on the power of visualization, positive thinking, and a strong inner belief.

He argued that by focusing your mind on wealth in a deliberate way, you can attract abundance into your life. Wattles introduced a fascinating concept: "There is a thinking stuff from which all things are made, and which, in its original state, permeates, penetrates, and fills the interspaces of the Universe. A thought in this substance produces the thing that is imaged by the thought." Isn't that incredible? A book that's now more than one hundred years old referenced the ability to use our thoughts to directly influence and shape our world. Wattles was truly ahead of his time.

Another influential book from this era is *Think and Grow Rich*, published in 1937 by Napoleon Hill. Hill interviewed more than five hundred successful individuals, including Henry Ford and Thomas Edison, and distilled their experiences into thirteen principles for success, with key components being faith, imagination, the subconscious mind, and the sixth sense.

Since then, countless individuals across various fields have used manifestation to achieve success and create their dream lives. One of my favorite examples is the story of the actor Jim Carrey, who has famously promoted manifestation, saying he is a huge visualizer and manifester. Before he became a household name, Carrey was a struggling comedian, barely making ends meet; he described how he wrote himself a check for ten million dollars for "acting services rendered," dating it Thanksgiving

1995. He then carried the check everywhere he went and would drive up to Mulholland Drive every night for four years, manifesting his life. And incredibly, just before Thanksgiving 1995, Carrey found out he was going to be paid ten million dollars for the role he had landed in the movie *Dumb and Dumber*.

As I delved into this new world, I found myself grappling with two opposing halves of my being. On one side, there was the part of me that had been blown wide open by my mystical experience. This part was excited by everything I was learning—and overwhelmed in a good way. I couldn't understand why everyone wasn't talking about this. Why wasn't this common knowledge?

On the other side, there was a healthy skeptic in me who needed proof and evidence. Coming from a traditional upbringing, the idea that our thoughts could somehow magically shape reality seemed far-fetched. I worried what others would think if I started talking about these ideas. Would they think I had lost my mind?

That's why I loved learning about the science behind manifestation, which we'll explore as we move through this chapter. I felt that I needed to find that proof, not just for myself, but to convince others, too. And I believe I have found it through years of learning, testing, failing, and trying every single day, as well as coaching hundreds of individual clients and seeing their results with my formula and technique.

As I dove deeper into the world of manifestation, one key concept came up again and again: the idea of conscious manifestation. It isn't enough to simply believe in the power of manifestation; to truly harness its potential, I needed to learn how to manifest consciously and intentionally.

Conscious Manifestation

Manifestation is the deliberate act of bringing your dreams, visions, and desires into physical reality through the power of your thoughts, emotions, beliefs, and actions. You could have a dream to manifest more money, find love, land the perfect job, become an author, build a successful business, or heal from a health condition—it can be anything, big or small. Conscious manifestation is a gradual process of becoming aware of your innate ability to shape your life and choosing to do it intentionally so that you can create anything you want.

However, as you'll learn more about in the next chapter, the paradox is that this requires you to get clear on your intention and actively start to embody it before it manifests. This means consciously aligning with your desire, moving beyond wanting, and getting out of a state of lack and into a state that is equal to the version of you who already lives that life.

Most people, likely including you right now, aren't manifesting consciously. By default, you create your reality based on your unconscious thoughts, beliefs, and patterns. You're reacting to life rather than consciously creating it. You're on autopilot, replaying old patterns and beliefs without realizing it. You think your thoughts are just background noise and don't recognize that you're the architect responsible for your reality.

In fact, research suggests that by age thirty-five, about 95 percent of our identity is composed of deeply ingrained patterns. These include our behaviors, emotional responses, subconscious habits, fixed attitudes, beliefs, and perceptions, which all operate automatically, much like a computer program, beyond our conscious recognition. This means that most people's subconscious patterns are the invisible puppet strings that shape their lives, influencing everything from finances, to relationships, to health and careers.

This is why so many people find themselves stuck in the same cycles, year after year, despite their best efforts to change. They might consciously want something different, but their subconscious programming keeps pulling them back to the familiar, manifesting the same circumstances in their lives.

For example, how often have you heard the following:

"I feel like I'm stuck in a rut. Every day feels the same, and I don't know how to break out of this cycle."

"No matter how hard I work, I can never get ahead financially. It's like I'm always struggling just to make ends meet."

"I keep attracting the same type of toxic relationships. I seem to be drawn to the same kind of people who let me down over and over again."

"Despite how hard I try, I've never got any money."

These patterns can show up in financial struggles, unfulfilling relationships, dead-end jobs, or health issues. You might feel like you're fighting an uphill battle, taking one step forward only to slide two steps back. Simply put, you're likely unaware of your subconscious beliefs and patterns running the show behind the scenes. You might consciously set goals and make plans, but if those goals don't align with your deeper programming, you'll continue to manifest the same unwanted results. This is like driving a car with one foot on the gas and the other on the brake. You might be pushing down on the accelerator, visualizing your destination and planning your route, but if your subconscious foot is pressing on the brake pedal, you won't get very far.

I'm not suggesting that you have "attracted" your hardships. This isn't about blame or shame. In fact, although you might be unconsciously manifesting, it doesn't mean you are responsible for the trauma or difficult circumstances in your life. This is a damaging thought that can lead to self-blame and guilt. Some people suffer beyond their control due to their surroundings, environment, or systemic issues. Not everyone's circumstances are a direct result of their thoughts and beliefs.

The good news is that the subconscious mind, much like a computer, can be reprogrammed at any time. By bringing your conscious awareness to your patterns and beliefs, you can begin to shift them in a new direction. You can start installing new beliefs, building new habits, and aligning your subconscious mind with your conscious goals. And as you do, you'll begin to see your external reality shift to match your internal state. You'll start attracting new opportunities, relationships, and levels of abundance that reflect your deepest beliefs and expectations.

That's the essence of conscious manifestation: it's not about forcing the world to bend to your will; instead, it's about aligning yourself with the life you desire from the inside out. In the upcoming chapters, you'll learn proven strategies for reprogramming your subconscious mind, cultivating supportive beliefs and emotions, and aligning your actions with your ultimate desires.

But before we delve into any form of change, we need to understand the deeper essence of manifestation. To do this, we'll first explore the very fabric of reality itself.

Everything Is Energy

When you look around, the world seems solid and tangible, doesn't it? The chair you're sitting on, the book in your hands, the ground beneath your feet—it all feels undeniably real and physical. But here's a surprising truth: this solidity is an illusion. At the deepest level, everything you see and touch is made up of intangible energy.

Quantum physics has blown the lid off our understanding of reality, revealing that our physical world is composed of energy, vibrating at varying frequencies to create what we perceive as solid forms. Everything within our experience—everything we see, hear, taste, smell, and touch—is a form of energy interacting in a vast, invisible field of intelligence. I know it sounds like something out of a sci-fi novel, but this is hard science.

Everything is energy, and from this energy, matter is formed. To really wrap your head around this concept and how it relates to your own manifestation journey, we need to start from the ground up, breaking down our physical world to understand its essence.

Imagine you've got a superpowered microscope, and you zoom in on your hand. At first, you'd see skin and layers of tissue, then diving deeper, cells. Keep going, and you'll come across molecules and then atoms, which are the building blocks of not just your body but also everything in the universe. Now, here's the wild part: atoms are more than 99.9 percent empty space, with invisible fields of energy. The fundamental structure of matter, the cornerstone of all that is tangible, is mostly . . . nothing. It's an empty stage where a tiny fraction of matter moves around, popping in and out of existence. But it gets even trippier. Zoom in again, below the atoms, and you'll hit the subatomic level, where particles like protons, neutrons, and electrons occupy a mere 0.01 percent of the atom's volume. The rest is a vast, invisible intelligence known as *quantum fields*. (More on quantum fields later.)

This means that the world you perceive with your senses is essentially energy. At this microscopic level, things get very strange. Instead of being solid, everything is more like waves of energy. Electrons and tiny particles don't sit still; they don't have a definite position. They exist as probabilities and spread out like ripples across a pond. This is the quantum realm, where the usual rules don't apply. Here, we discover that observation affects reality, and possibilities exist in multiple states until they're measured or observed. This understanding is crucial for manifestation because it reveals how consciousness—your thoughts and observations—can influence physical reality at its most fundamental level.

The bottom line is this: at your core, you are energy, and so is the thing you seek to manifest. They are both part of the same infinite, invisible field. In my journey, this realization sparked two big questions: If everything is energy, where does it come from? And more importantly, is there a way to work with this energy field so I can manifest a specific outcome in my life?

Understanding the Universe

As I delved deeper into the question of our origins, I discovered that many ancient traditions and modern scientific theories point to the existence of a Universal energy field that connects all things. Whether known as the Universe, the Quantum Field, the Unified Field, the Source, the Universal Mind, or the Divine Matrix, the underlying principle remains the same: this field is the foundation of all energy and the bedrock of manifestation. The name you choose to call it doesn't matter; what's important is that the concept resonates with you.

In this book, when I refer to the "Universe" in the context of manifestation, I'm talking about this all-encompassing energy field. I might use different names interchangeably throughout, but they all point to this fundamental essence.

Now, let's ponder this together. If we are all part of this vast energy field, and because our thoughts and emotions are also forms of energy, it's conceivable that we could consciously interact with this field to manifest our desires. By focusing on our intentions with aligned emotions and actions, can we influence the Quantum Realm to create our reality?

Physicists tell us that the basic components of matter are not individual particles but rather a continuous, fluidlike substance known as quantum fields. Quantum field theory suggests that this field underpins the entire Universe, permeating all space and time. This means that everything in our physical world—every particle, atom, molecule, and object in the Universe—can be understood as energy, vibration, or even a ripple within the quantum field.

To make this tangible, imagine for a moment that what you want to manifest already exists as pure energy. You can't see it, you can't feel it, and it definitely might feel separate from you. But is it? If the quantum field contains infinite energy and everything derives from this field, then, in theory, every possibility already exists; it's already "out there," waiting to materialize into form.

Before you get too excited, I want you to remember that the Universe operates solely in the "now"—the eternal present moment. Every time you look at the clock, it doesn't show you a future time—it's always now. This fundamental truth is crucial to grasp. The now is all there is and ever will be, emphasizing that the sense of "want" when we desire an outcome stems from the illusion of separation and a fixation on a future point.

By understanding this, you'll recognize that manifestation is about bridging the gap between what you desire and who you are "being" in the present moment. This means that the Universe doesn't simply grant our wishes in a direct transaction; instead, it mirrors what we embody and projects it in the present moment.

The Universe exists in a dimension far removed from our concept of time. It doesn't differentiate between "past" and "future" or see the gaps between objects as we do, hence why "wanting" projects a vibration of "lack," only drawing more "wanting" into your life.

When we ask for something, the Universe always says yes. It can be no other way. When you casually say, "I want more money," the Universe affirms, "Yes!" and you'll experience more "wanting" of more money. When you state, "I just want to be happy," the Universe agrees, and you'll find yourself continuing to chase the desire for happiness. When you say, "I want a loving partner," the Universe affirms, "Yes!" and you'll find yourself waiting for love, constantly seeking it outside yourself. When you say, "I want to lose weight," the Universe agrees, and you'll experience an increased fixation on your perceived lack of fitness or ideal body image. Maybe you say, "I want a better job," so the Universe aligns with your state of being and you'll find yourself continually desiring a more fulfilling career, repeatedly checking new job listings, or feeling unfulfilled and undervalued in your professional life.

Now, let's flip the script. When you say, "I am surrounded by love and amazing relationships," the Universe starts to mirror your new state of being, and you'll attract loving, supportive people into your life. You'll find yourself appreciating the love that already exists around you and cultivating a sense of self-love that attracts even more love from others.

When you start saying, "I am healthy, strong, and vibrant," the Universe aligns with your vibration, and you'll begin to make choices that support your well-being. You'll find yourself naturally drawn to nourishing foods, enjoyable physical activities, and a more balanced lifestyle.

Just to note, though, I am not saying that by declaring, "I am a millionaire," millions will immediately start flowing your way. This is a game of vibrational resonance. This field of intelligence doesn't just hand out desires in our own concept of time; it happens when your energy matches the energy of your intentions.

In my experience, some of my manifestations have felt instantaneous, within a few days or weeks. Some of my most significant manifestations have taken a little longer, but they've all happened, most of the time in ways that I couldn't possibly imagine how.

Now that you have grasped that we are all part of this vast, interconnected field, it begs the question: What kind of energy are you putting out into the Universe? Are you aware of the vibrations that you are emitting with your thoughts, emotions, and actions? And more importantly, are these vibrations in alignment with what you truly desire to manifest?

How to Consciously Manifest

If everything is energy, then we, as human beings, are also energetic, vibrational beings. We emit a unique vibration. It's like we are walking, talking radio towers, broadcasting our personal energy signal into the Universe at every moment. I see this energy broadcast as everything that encompasses us: our thoughts, feelings, behaviors, habits, personality traits, health, and more. Are you conscious of the signal you send out?

To understand our personal signal, let's consider vibration as information. Your vibration—the energy you emit—is broadcasting data about your state of being to the Universe. It's your energetic "I am" statement. When you're in a state of wanting, the message you're sending out is one of lack. You're effectively saying, "I am someone who doesn't have what I desire." This vibration, or energetic signature, then attracts more experiences that match this state of lack.

On the flip side, when you embody the feeling of already having what you desire, you're broadcasting a completely different signal. You're saying, "I am someone who is fulfilled, who has what they need." This shift in your energetic communication changes everything. The Universe responds not to what you want, but to the information you're broadcasting through your thoughts, feelings, and actions.

In this context, we can think of frequency as how often this energetic message is being broadcast. Higher frequencies are associated with more positive, uplifting states of being, while lower frequencies relate to heavier, more negative states. When you're feeling grateful, joyful, or abundant, you're operating at a higher frequency, sending out positive vibrations. Conversely, when you're stuck in a state of lack or wanting, you're at a lower frequency, repeatedly broadcasting details of scarcity.

I see manifestation as a process, a gradual shift of moving my personal vibration into alignment with what I seek. For example, in 2019, I always lacked money. I never had it. I made enough of it, but it always slipped through my fingers. I was constantly complaining, worrying, working out my expenses, and spending in my head. And then, when I learned the process you're about to read, I slowly became aligned with the abundance of money. I did this by starting to appreciate the smallest amount of money I had and committing to a daily gratitude practice, thanking the Universe for money before I had it. It seemed like such a paradox to say thank you before receiving it, but somehow, it worked.

Whenever I'm coaching, I like to use the radio analogy to explain this gradual shift in vibration. Let's imagine you decide to listen to a specific station on an old radio. You start by thinking about the station; let's call this your intention. You intend to listen to Radio 1 here in the UK, which resonates at 97.9 FM. To tune in, you start in lack with crackles and white noise; you gradually move through the dial until, bingo, you pick up the station.

That's the essence of manifestation: you start in lack and gradually build up resonance to match the frequency of your desires.

This is where the Law of Attraction comes into play. This universal principle states that like attracts like—the vibration we send out into the world draws back to us experiences and circumstances that resonate at the same frequency. In other words, our external reality reflects our internal state. The Law of Attraction is always at work, whether we're aware of it or not, constantly shaping our lives based on the energy we emit.

It's not enough to simply think positively and hope for the best, though. The Law of Attraction is just the beginning. It lays the foundations for manifestation, yet the process goes much deeper. True manifestation requires us to actively embody the energy of what we want and participate fully in creating our desired reality by taking aligned action. It's a joint creative process between our inner world and the Universe.

Here's an example. Let's say you are reading this book to manifest love. You start by visualizing yourself in the perfect relationship, feeling the love, joy, and happiness that comes with it. You engage in practices like meditation, journaling, gratitude, and walking around as if you're already in that relationship. Your entire state of being shifts from wanting love to embodying love. As you commit to doing this daily and consciously focus your thoughts, emotions, and actions on the love you desire, you create a specific vibration in the quantum field. This vibration ripples out, interacting with and influencing the energy around you. It's like throwing a pebble into a calm pond—the ripples spread out, affecting the entire surface of the water.

However, just like a single pebble creates only a small disturbance, a fleeting thought or momentary feeling of love may not create a strong enough vibration to manifest your desires. To create significant change, you need to consistently focus on your intention and stay tuned in. Imagine repeatedly throwing pebbles into the pond, always aiming for the same spot. The ripples grow stronger with each pebble, reinforcing and amplifying one another.

The more you focus on embodying the energy of love, or any other desire, the stronger your vibration becomes in the quantum field. At a certain point, your vibration reaches a critical amplitude and begins to resonate with the vibration of love that already exists in the Universe. This is where the magic of resonance comes into play.

Resonance occurs when two vibrations are synchronized and amplify each other. It's like singing a note and hearing someone match your pitch perfectly—both voices naturally align and create a stronger, harmonious sound. When your vibration of love resonates with the vibration of love in the Universe, you create a powerful, energetic vortex that attracts more of the same energy. This resonance draws in other people, circumstances, and opportunities that are aligned with the love you desire. It's as if the Universe conspires to bring you the perfect match, orchestrating synchronicities and serendipitous encounters.

Manifestation is a continuous process of aligning your energy with your desires. The key is maintaining your vibration of love, even in the face of challenges or temporary setbacks. You need to commit to doing this work every single day. By consistently showing up and doing the inner work, you send a clear signal to the Universe that you are in alignment with your intentions and ready to receive the outcomes you desire.

As you continue to resonate with love, the energy grows stronger, reaching a tipping point where it can no longer be contained in the realm of possibility and it spills over into your physical reality, manifesting as the loving relationship that you've been visualizing. Your outer world begins to mirror your inner state of being as the Universe brings you the experiences that match your vibration.

If this example is of someone consciously manifesting love, what about all the other thoughts, emotions, and beliefs that subtly run behind our conscious awareness? Do these also communicate with the Universe? This leads us to a powerful and perhaps even unsettling question: How much of your reality is being shaped by your thoughts, emotions, and beliefs that lie beyond your conscious observation? And if you were to bring the light of conscious observation to these hidden patterns, would it change the way you experience your world?

The Observer Effect

Earlier in this chapter, we explored the idea that everything in the Universe, including you and me, is made up of energy. We learned that even the most solid-seeming objects are composed of tiny, vibrating particles. Now, let's dive into the behavior of these particles. In the quantum world, particles can act in two seemingly opposite ways: like waves and like particles.

First, let's consider the "wave" aspect. Imagine dropping a pebble into a calm pond. The ripples that spread out from the point of impact are like waves of energy. These waves move through the water, exploring all possible paths and directions. Now, let's consider the "particle" aspect. Imagine the same pebble you dropped into the pond. The pebble is like a particle—a tiny, localized unit of matter. When particles behave like particles, they have a definite location and can be measured and observed directly, just as you can perceive the pebble's position in the pond.

However, in the quantum world, particles can switch between behaving like waves (ripples on a pond) and behaving like particles (the pebble itself), depending on how we observe them. When scientists are not looking at a particle, it behaves like a wave, spreading out and exploring all possible paths, like the ripples on the pond. But the moment they observe it, the wave-like behavior collapses and the particle appears in a single, definite location, like the pebble in the pond. This might seem strange, but it's been confirmed by countless experiments and is a fundamental principle of quantum mechanics.

One of these experiments, the double-slit experiment, was a real "aha!" moment for me. It was the icing on the cake, the cherry on top, the moment when everything clicked into place. Imagine you have a barrier with two parallel slits cut into it, and you're firing a beam of tiny particles, like electrons, at this barrier. On the other side of the barrier is a screen recording where the particles land. Now, if the particles behaved only like solid objects, you'd expect to see two distinct clusters of impacts on the screen, directly in line with the two slits. It would be like firing a bullet through two holes in a wall and seeing two bullet holes on the other side. However, when this experiment is conducted, something extraordinary happens.

Instead of bullet holes, the particles form a striped pattern on the screen, which looks like the ripples you'd see when dropping two pebbles into a calm pond. This pattern suggests that the electrons are behaving like waves, spreading out and interfering with each other, just like ocean waves. Now, here's where it gets even stranger: when scientists placed detectors near the slits to observe which slit each particle passed through, the striped pattern disappeared altogether and the particles started behaving like individual solid bullets, forming two distinct clusters on the screen behind. It's as if the particles "knew" they were being watched and changed their behavior accordingly! The act of observation caused the wave of energy to collapse into physical matter. In quantum mechanics, this is called *collapse of the wave function.*

Learning this blew my mind. It immediately made sense. The outcome mirrored so much of the work I witness with my clients. When I ask them to start consciously visualizing and embodying a new future, almost like magic, a cascade of opportunities start to appear. "Matt, you're not going to believe it," they say. Or, "Matt, it came out of the blue." I get this all the time. But why? Could it be that the act of their own observation toward a new future causes it to collapse from mere potential into their reality? Now, I'm no quantum physicist, and I tread lightly when drawing parallels between the microcosmic behaviors of particles and our macro lives. Yet what I witness daily is far too powerful to ignore.

If you're drawing conclusions similar to mine, then here's the key question: We know that observation affects particles at the subatomic level, the very building blocks of our reality. Could this fundamental principle extend beyond the laboratory? When we focus our attention on a desired future, as I've witnessed with countless clients, are we essentially collapsing waves of possibility into tangible reality? Could the same principles that govern quantum behavior explain the mechanics of manifestation? Think about it: when we fully commit to our vision and embody that future with every cell of our being through feeling, believing, and acting as if it's already here, we're doing exactly what those scientists observe in their experiments—collapsing waves of possibility into physical reality through the power of focused observation. Could this be the key to manifesting the life we desire?

PRACTICE:

Collapse of the Wave Game

In this practice, you will "collapse the wave" by manifesting something into your reality during the next forty-eight hours. To do this, choose something small that you can set without becoming attached to the outcome—for example, someone buying you a coffee, finding unexpected money, receiving an uplifting compliment, getting an unexpected pay raise, or someone asking you out on a date. Once you've set the intention, let it go completely, allowing the Universe to take care of the "how" and "when."

Here's how to practice it:

Step 1: Choose Your Intention

Pick an intention that both excites you and feels small enough to forget. The key is to choose an outcome that you can envision without too much skepticism.

Step 2: Write It Down

In a journal, with pen and paper, or in a notes app on your phone, write down the date and time as if it were forty-eight hours from now. Set your writing in the present tense as if it has already manifested. Write it like this: "I am so grateful that [write your intention] unfolded in my life because [write how it made you feel]. Thank you, thank you, thank you." For example: "I am so grateful that I received unexpected money because it made me feel excited and abundantly blessed. Thank you, thank you, thank you."

Step 3: Visualize and Feel It

Slowly read your intention back to yourself. Now, close your eyes and imagine this intention unfolding in your life, while also tuning in to how it would feel. This might be gratitude, love, relief, or peace. Sit with the intention and feeling for at least one minute. The goal is to strike a balance between the vision and the feeling, connecting with the outcome as if it has already happened.

Step 4: Set and Forget

Having set your intention and connected with it emotionally, release your grip on it and send it out to the Universe. Your job is now to relax and trust that the Universe will handle the "how" and "when" of it coming to fruition.

Step 5: Review
After forty-eight hours, revisit your journal. Whether or not your intention has manifested, review your written words and reflect on any occurrences, synchronicities, or feelings that relate to your desire.

Now that you have completed this practice, continue your life as usual. I frequently try these experiments with my community, so check my Instagram (@MattCookeCoach) to read other comments.

In my experience, having seen hundreds of thousands of people try these experiments and having read thousands of their comments, I've noticed a pattern: some people report their intention manifesting within a few days, while others mention that even if it didn't happen within the specified time frame, it eventually manifested when they least expected it.

As you may have noticed, in this practice, we don't focus on wanting the outcome; instead, we visualize it and feel it as if it had already happened. This subtle shift from wanting to being is the key to true manifestation. When we want something, we inadvertently emphasize the lack of it in our lives. However, when we visualize and feel the desired outcome, we align our energy with the reality we wish to create.

CHAPTER 2

From Wanting to Being

While on vacation in Corfu with Corisande, I was confronted with "wanting" in its rawest form. It was a rare break from work, and I was lying in the sunshine, reflecting on our life. It was a mess; we were deeply unhappy in our corporate jobs, money was tight, debt was mounting up, and life felt like a never-ending race on a treadmill. To make things worse, the company Corisande and I worked for was reorganizing its structure—a less frightening term for "going under." We desperately wanted to be free from all the stress and pressure.

As I looked out at the most stunning view, my mind was elsewhere; the beauty of the present moment was lost in the whirlwind of my fearful thoughts. There I was in paradise, yet my "wanting" of something else was stealing and squeezing the joy out of my life. Then the paradox hit me: constantly wanting more equaled the lack in my life. I remember saying to myself,

"Wanting is the problem." Want is like a caged animal, pacing, desperate for freedom. With each passing second, frustration swells inside you. The more you want, the more you realize what you don't have. In this relentless pursuit of what we want, we trap ourselves in a cycle of never-ending desire, stuck in an infinite loop, leaving an unbearable feeling of lack and separation.

I realized my whole life had become a relentless pursuit; the constant want had become my identity. Every achievement and milestone was a fleeting moment before the next want emerged. In this cycle, life felt like climbing an endless staircase—always moving but never progressing. I was the youngest manager at a firm of real estate agents, reaching the top of the ladder at just twenty-six years old. I was "successful" on paper, but deep down, I felt insecure. I craved more—more money, more safety, and more security. I had believed that climbing to the top would make my problems disappear, but it didn't. Despite my achievements, I still wanted more and was stuck in a never-ending cycle of lack. Corisande felt the same way, trapped in her own version of this exhausting pursuit.

Over time, this relentless cycle affected our overall well-being, leading to feelings of emptiness. It was as if we were characters in a story written by societal expectations who were chasing a narrative of success and fulfillment that eluded us at every turn. I remember thinking that all of our previous accomplishments had become stepping stones to the next goal, leaving us feeling incomplete.

And as if that wasn't enough, our jobs were hanging by a thread. This was wanting in its rawest form—a constant longing for something more, something just beyond the horizon, a void that no achievement seemed to fill. This was my wake-up call, a hard slap of reality. All the chasing, all the grinding during the years wasn't filling the void or patching over the disappointment, emptiness, and insecurity. I told myself, "I've got to change this; I need to try something different."

Later that evening, Corisande and I sat on a beautiful terrace overlooking the ocean, watching the sunset, drinking cocktails, and laughing. It was one of those moments I wanted to bottle; it was simple yet beautiful. It felt as though our life in England did not exist; we were on the cusp of having no jobs, yet life felt perfect. We were fully immersed in the present, time had slipped away, and we were relaxed, in a trancelike state, imagining this moment was our reality. In that moment we found clarity. Looking at each other, we knew. "Let's just bite the bullet and quit our jobs. Let's just be free," I said. We had tasted freedom and were hungry for it.

We had no proper plan—just a shared dream to spend our days together, a side hustle in digital marketing, and a firm belief in the concept of manifestation. It felt like the whole year had been gearing me up for this. Here was our opening to take a leap of faith and start living our best life.

After this moment of clarity, I was struck by a profound realization: I had misunderstood the essence of manifestation for months. So many of us set goals that, despite our desires, feel perpetually out of reach or steeped in lack. But this journey was no longer about *wanting* to be free; I needed to *become* free.

So, that's what we did. When we landed back in England, we submitted our two-month notice to resign from our corporate jobs. There was no safety net; we had a mortgage, car payments, and debt up to our ears. We even took out another loan to cover the bills for six months. On paper, it looked like madness—my inner "animal" was in turmoil, questioning what people would think, fretting over the mortgage and the improbability of making a living online and replacing our traditional income.

One thing was crystal clear, though: we were suddenly free. Mondays became the highlight of our week, with no more Sunday-night dread and that sick feeling in the pit of my stomach. We had all the time in the world to sit with our laptops in Starbucks and dream up our future. It was incredible, a taste of true bliss. After years of being trapped in the corporate rat race, we were free of it all. The constant emails, the daily grind—it had all stopped. That feeling was priceless.

Although quitting our jobs and taking out a loan might not seem sensible on paper, the preceding months had laid a foundation of belief and readiness within us. It was as though everything had conspired to prepare us for this leap of faith. I realized that to manifest our dream life, it wasn't enough to chase the idea of freedom—we needed to embody it. I had to become the person already living that free, manifested future, aligning my current self with that vision.

The Paradox of Want

Have you ever wanted something so badly, only to feel that the more you want it, the farther away it becomes? You put all your energy into it, but somehow, it always feels just out of reach. And when you eventually get what you want, another "want" typically emerges.

You're likely reading this book because you want something. If it's nothing specific, it may be more about wanting a feeling, such as happiness, security, freedom, love, or peace. Whether it's something specific, a feeling, or simply an intuitive pull that you need to change, go there in your mind. Sit with that desire. What is it that you really want? Why do you want it? What comes up as you think about this want? How does that feel in your body?

In the journey of manifestation, many of us find ourselves entangled in this exact paradox trap, where the act of wanting intensifies the experience of lack. As a result, the experience we attract is more lack. This is the crux of the paradox: when you obsess over something you want, you unconsciously reflect deficiency—a gap between your current state and your desired state. One could say, in theory, you are observing your lack without even realizing, and I would theorize that this observation is repeatedly collapsing the same outcomes. Considering that the Law of Attraction states that like attracts like, it makes sense that wanting attracts more wanting unless you move beyond it.

The dictionary defines *want* as "The state or condition of not having something; the absence or deficiency of something. A desire for something. To lack or be short of something desirable or essential." Take a moment to let that sink in. Now, imagine for a moment that your deepest desire has already manifested. How does that make you feel? Anxious? Frustrated? Deficient? Or perhaps in lack? Of course it won't; you'll feel the complete opposite: at peace, in love with life, grateful, excited, relieved, content, and happy. The dictionary's definition of *want*, therefore, literally reflects this truth. Wanting is the problem.

Most of us aren't fully tuned in to the vibrational frequency we send out. It's a common human slip; we get caught up focusing on what we lack or what's missing from our lives, waiting for a future event to allow us to feel a certain way. At times, we're all guilty of not fully realizing that this focus subtly broadcasts a frequency of scarcity into the Universe.

This is the heart of the paradox. Most people live in a state of lack, desperately wanting something outside of them to change how they feel inside. But this contradicts the essence of true manifestation and stems from a misunderstanding of how energy and attraction work. The reality is that when we want something intensely, we emit a vibration of lack, a subtle message to the Universe that we are without what we desire. This vibration doesn't attract what we want; instead, it attracts the absence of it, resulting in only more lack. The Universe responds to what you are, what you feel, and what you embody, not what you want. The key to successful manifestation, then, is not to want but to be.

I know what you might be thinking: "But Matt, isn't it natural to want things? Isn't that what drives us to pursue our goals and dreams in the first place?" Absolutely. But there's a difference between a healthy want and the kind of want that keeps us trapped in lack.

A healthy want comes from a place of inspiration, excitement, and alignment. When used correctly, it's an incredible motivator. It's the kind of wanting that feels expansive and energizing, like a spark that ignites your passion and purpose. This type of desire is often accompanied by a sense of trust and faith, a knowing that your dreams are on their way to you. On the other hand, the wanting that keeps us stuck often comes from a place of fear, desperation, or a sense that we're not good enough as we are. It's the kind of wanting that feels contracted, heavy, constricting, and draining.

The most important question you can ever ask yourself is: "What do *I* really want?" That's not what society expects you to want, not what you think you should want based on others' success, and not what you've been conditioned to believe you need. This question cuts through external influences to reach your authentic desires. When you form an answer from genuine self-awareness rather than comparison or envy, everything shifts. Your thoughts, feelings, actions, and choices naturally align with your true vision. The Universe then begins to cocreate with you, mirroring your authentic state of being, and your external world transforms to reflect this new vision.

As you tune your awareness and state of being to become aligned with the future version of yourself who already has what you seek—especially when your want comes from a place of inspiration—you go from wanting to having, or more precisely, to being. This shift transforms lack into abundance, separation into wholeness. By *being*, I mean embodying the state of already having what you desire in the present moment. As you focus on being in alignment, living as if your desired future has already manifested, you close the gap between wanting and having. And that, right there, is the art of mastering the paradox.

This shift fundamentally contradicts our habitual programming, which is wired to believe that effort, struggle, and force are the paths to achievement. Manifestation and the Universe operate on energy, vibration, frequency, resonance, and alignment. By adopting the emotional state of the future you wish to create, you align yourself with that reality; your vibration goes from unconsciously repelling and blocking to consciously allowing and receiving.

For example, if you pause and observe the world around you, you'll notice how frequently phrases like "I want more money," "I want a better job," or "I just want to be happy" are used in everyday conversations. Turning this observation inward, you might say, "I just want success," or "I want to find love." These seemingly innocuous statements reveal a deeper undercurrent of waiting for fulfillment in some distant future.

But what if the true arrival of what we seek is here and now, in the journey itself rather than the destination?

Shifting Perspective into the Present Moment

There's an ancient Persian tale that perfectly illustrates how wanting can blind us to the abundance already present in our lives. Ali Hafed was a wealthy farmer who lived not far from the Indus River. He had a beautiful family, land, and animals. He was content with life, or so it seemed. One day, out of the blue, a wise old Buddhist priest paid him a visit. The priest told stories about diamonds and how diamond mines were being discovered across nearby lands. He said, "A single stone could make a man rich beyond his wildest dreams." He told Hafed that if he had just one diamond the size of his thumb, he could purchase the county, and if he had a mine of diamonds, he could place his children upon thrones through the influence of their great wealth.

Hafed was immediately sold on the idea. All he wanted now was his own diamond mine to complete his life. He told his family, "As soon as I find my own mine, we can finally relax and enjoy our wealth." So with the seed of desire in his mind, he sold his farm, left his family behind, and set out on a quest to find diamonds.

He traveled far and wide, searching for diamonds in many countries. His journey took him through the Middle East and across Europe. By the time he arrived in Barcelona, Spain, he was a broken man, exhausted and penniless, with no single diamond to his name. He was defeated; the dream of "wanting" his own diamond mine had beaten him. With no other hope and not wanting to return empty-handed, he threw himself into the sea between the Pillars of Hercules, never to be seen again.

Meanwhile, back at the farm, the new owner was casually leading his camel down to the stream on the land. Out of nowhere, while enjoying the moment, the new farmer noticed a flash of light from the corner of his eye. He looked down into the stream and saw an unusual black stone shimmering as it clashed with rays of sunshine. He reached in, picked it up, and turned it over in his hands. He didn't think anything of it except how unusual it was, so he put it into his pocket, carried it home, and placed it on his mantelpiece for safekeeping.

A few days later, the wise priest paid the farm another visit. This time, while talking with the new owner, his eyes caught the black stone on the mantelpiece. With a gasp of recognition, he rushed over to examine it more closely. "Do you know what this is?" he asked the farmer, his voice trembling with excitement. "This is an unpolished diamond! One of the largest I have ever seen!" The farmer was stunned. He had been living with a fortune on his mantelpiece and hadn't even realized it.

Together, the priest and the farmer rushed outside to the garden and quickly discovered that the streambed was covered in diamonds. It turned out that Ali Hafed had been sitting on a literal diamond mine the whole time. This discovery led to the famous Golconda diamond mines, some of the most magnificent in all human history.

The story of Ali Hafed is a powerful reminder of the abundance often hidden in plain sight. It illustrates how our relentless pursuit of what we want can blind us to the abundance already present in our lives. We become so focused on chasing after what we want, we fail to appreciate what we already have.

If Hafed had stopped and appreciated the wealth already in his life, he wouldn't have felt the need to chase after more. In fact, by embracing a state of being aligned with abundance, he would have eventually stumbled upon the diamonds on his own land. In the context of manifestation, he would have manifested the diamonds without going anywhere else. Ultimately, wanting the diamonds equated to his own lack, leading to separation from his family, a void of loneliness, and a gap between where he was and the wealth he sought—it was all an illusion that no amount of distance could fill.

As I'm writing this, it's a Sunday afternoon in April in Cornwall, England. The sun is out, and a bumble bee is gently humming alongside my right ear while collecting pollen; it's simple yet beautiful. My younger self would have unconsciously ignored this moment. But why am I telling you this? Because, just like you, there is something I really, really want. I want this book to be a bestseller and be in the hands of millions of people across the globe, not for egotistic reasons, but for purpose. The thought that one day, millions of people worldwide might improve their lives through my book lights me up. It fills my heart with love. But why should I wait for the announcement from *The New York Times* to feel those emotions? Why do I need to stay in lack until some distant future? Can the same level of love be found right now? You might not realize this, but at this very moment, if you search for it, you can cultivate the same emotions that would equal your future manifestation coming to fruition. My message is: Why wait? What if the secret is opening your eyes and seeing the diamonds around you?

As you embrace the emotions now, you naturally increase your vibrational frequency, which, in turn, becomes aligned with what you want. As a result, you dissolve the wanting paradox and attract what you want! That leads me to another question: What if what you seek isn't separate from you? What if your deepest desire is here right now, on a frequency of energy invisible to your senses?

The Illusion of Separation

At the heart of wanting something lies the illusion that you are separate from it. When we believe that we are separate from our desires, we create a sense of distance, empty space, a rift between where we are right now and what we want. But here's the truth: everything in the Universe is interconnected. The quantum field, that invisible sea of energy we explored in the previous chapter, has no gaps or empty spaces. It's a continuous web of energy, vibration, and information that connects us all, even if we can't perceive it with our physical senses. This means that you are connected to your deepest desires and wildest dreams right now.

Picture it like this: Imagine you're standing at the edge of a deep canyon. On the other side, you can see your dream life—a life filled with abundance, joy, and love. The gap between where you are and what you want seems impossibly wide, a void you could only hope to cross. But what if I told you that there's an invisible bridge spanning that distance? A bridge that's been there all along, just waiting for you to take the first step?

In the movie *Indiana Jones and the Last Crusade*, there's a scene in which the main character, Indy, must cross a seemingly impossible gulf to reach the Holy Grail. His faith is tested as he steps out into what appears to be thin air. But as he takes that leap of faith, his foot lands on an invisible bridge that carries him safely to the other side.

This relates to how most of us initially view the gap between our current reality and our desired future—as a void, a lack, an absence of what we want. However, the truth is that the bridge is there all along, just like the invisible bridge right in front of you. Indy's initial perception of the chasm was an illusion, a trick of the senses; however, his belief in the unknown made the bridge visible.

Once we grasp that the "space" between where we are and

what we want isn't separate from us, we realize that it's more like an invisible bridge. This is a powerful metaphor for how manifestation truly works. The bridge connecting you to your desires is always there, even when you can't see it. Your job is to trust in its existence, to have faith that the Universe is working in your favor, even when your physical senses tell you otherwise.

I experienced this firsthand six months after my wife and I left our corporate jobs. Our money was about to completely run dry, and my new digital marketing business was just scraping by. With mortgage payments and bills looming, I had a choice to make. Option A was to give in to the fear, admit defeat, and crawl back to my former industry, begging for a job and hoping that someone would take pity on me before the bills were due at the beginning of the following month. Option B was to trust in the invisible bridge, lean in to the fear, surrender my anxiety, and continue my meditation practice, visualizing the success of my online business. It meant continuing my daily gratitude practice; thanking the Universe for money, even when I had none; and consciously reframing my negative self-talk despite my overwhelming nerves.

But here's the thing—I had a vision for my life that kept me going, even in the darkest moments. And so, with a leap of faith and no clue how I would make it work, I chose Option B. I leaned in to the unknown and trusted that the Universe had my back. This time, though, and for the first time in six months, I stopped "wanting" to make it work. I gave it over to the Universe. It immediately felt like a weight had been lifted off my shoulders. I started being Matt of the future, someone who had already made it work. Of course, a part of me was screaming, "This is delusional, Matt, you are going to lose everything you have worked so hard to build." But I thought, what's the worst that's going to happen? That I beg the mortgage company for some extra time?

Little did I know that just a few weeks later, the world would shut down due to the COVID-19 pandemic. Within two weeks, my mortgage company, bank, and car finance company all reached out to offer payment breaks. It was a lifeline I couldn't have predicted, but it bought me the time I needed to turn my online business around.

In the months that followed, my internet business exploded. By the time my payments were due, I was earning more than I ever had in my former job. That's the magic of manifestation—it often catches you off guard, coming from the most unexpected places. My entire life turned around by trusting in the unseen and believing that the Universe is always conspiring in my favor.

Looking back, I'm humbled by how life unfolds in unexpected ways. That period showed me that even in our darkest times, there can be paths forward. While acknowledging the profound challenges and losses many faced, my experience taught me about trusting in possibilities, even when they're not yet visible. If I hadn't taken that leap of faith, I wouldn't be where I am today.

The key to dissolving the wanting paradox lies in aligning your inner world with your desires. This isn't about "faking it till you make it," but rather "feeling it till you make it." By showing up each day and mentally rehearsing your future as if it's already your reality, you train your body to vibrate at the frequency of your dreams. When I meditate, I slow down my brain waves and immerse myself in the sensations and emotions of my desired future.

My body responds as if it's happening: my heart rate speeds up with excitement, my muscles relax, and I enter a state of pure bliss; my entire body is living in that future, in the present moment. In a way, I am giving my body a taste of what it would feel like to live in my desired reality before it has manifested.

This is the magic of manifestation: By aligning your inner world with your desires, you create a shift in your outer world. By feeling the emotions of your dreams in the present moment, you collapse the illusion of time and space that seems to separate you from what you want. It's like you're already on that invisible bridge, confidently walking toward your dreams. The more you do this, the more natural and effortless it becomes, until one day, you look around and realize that your outer world has begun to match your inner vision.

Super Bobby

During the twelfth coaching session with my client Bobby, the CEO of an artificial intelligence start-up tackling data decay in the health-care industry, he showed up as usual, but something was visibly different this time. Pale, anxious, and noticeably shaken, he was clearly worried about something. We had an incredible three months of working together so far. He was beginning to see the magic of manifestation in his life and was gaining a good grasp on the fundamentals of what I teach. With two hundred fifty thousand dollars successfully raised from investors, Bobby was on the edge of significant breakthroughs with his tech start-up. Then, suddenly, Bobby faced a major problem. The Universe threw a massive test at him: the engineering team needed an additional one hundred seventy thousand dollars within a week to complete his project, or they would have to pull engineers off the job. Worse still, payroll was due, and he didn't have the funds.

Bobby was a bundle of nerves. He said, "This is why start-ups fail. I'm going to let everyone down who believes in me." He could barely catch a breath, let alone listen to me. I could tell that his mind was all over the place and his dream was teetering on the edge. We all can relate to moments like this. We work so hard on something and put our all into it, only for the rug to be pulled out from under us. This was Bobby's test. Could he silence the voice of doubt and do the work?

I was confident he could pull it off. By that point, I'd seen plenty of other clients face their own challenges. But here's the thing: instead of treating these challenges as setbacks, I saw them for what they were—moments of truth. These tests have a way of shining a light in the dark, revealing the very obstacles holding us back. For Bobby, it was all about recognizing his own strength, resilience, and worthiness. Those were the hurdles he needed to clear to unlock the success he was after.

So, I asked Bobby a simple question: "What do you want?"

He answered, "Two hundred fifty thousand dollars to pay the staff and engineers so they can finish the product." But here came the paradox. Expressing this want, Bobby found himself in a state of lack—the very principle we had been working to move beyond. Bobby was emitting a signal of "I do not have."

Despite the overwhelming circumstances, including a pregnant wife and two young children depending on him, Bobby understood the concept. Yet the practical application seemed elusive, especially when faced with such a complex and time-sensitive problem.

So, we took a deep breath and stepped back. I guided Bobby to observe his current state—overwhelmed, stressed, anxious, afraid—and then asked him to compare it with a future version of himself who has manifested what he wants.

This is when "Super Bobby" was born—a version of him that embodied all he wished to become. "Describe Super Bobby to me," I prompted. Bobby closed his eyes and guided me through a scene where Super Bobby was already living in this future state. His answer painted a picture of a strong, calm, and collected man, a figure of success who had effortlessly closed his investment round with confidence and pride. "Alright," I began, "how does Super Bobby hold himself?" Bobby's response: "He stands tall, in control, confident; he's on top of the pedestal." Then I moved to another question: "How does this feel?" Bobby replied, "It feels amazing. It's so exciting, relieving, and very freeing. I'm so happy." Then, I asked him to open his eyes.

"Bobby," I began, "why can you be consumed by fear one moment and in the next, feel free?" I explained that through certain practices like meditation or visualization, we can access deeper levels of our mind. In these states, our imagination becomes incredibly powerful. When we vividly picture a scenario, our brain and body can respond as if it's actually happening. This means that by visualizing himself as Super Bobby, he could experience the emotions and confidence of that version of himself, even before any external circumstances had changed.

I continued to explain the two choices Bobby had: Option A,

you can continue to fight, force, and chase the result you seek in your current state, or Option B, you can surrender to what's happening and move from wanting to being, embodying the essence of Super Bobby. To do this, you will need to consciously control your body's instinct to go into survival mode. You'll need to get present, close your eyes, block out the noise from the outside world, and meditate on being Super Bobby. Then, you are going to need to walk around and start thinking, feeling, and behaving like him.

By this point, Bobby had so much faith in this work that he was willing to listen. He agreed to show up every day, embodying Super Bobby. He wasn't being ignorant of the situation before him; he was embodying a new personality. Instead of being in fear, Bobby's task was to be grateful for unexpected money before it was made manifest.

After our session, Bobby went silent for a month and I lost contact with him. Despite the radio silence, I knew he was onto something; I didn't doubt him once. One month later, Bobby attended our call, and his life had turned around. Before I could speak, Bobby said, "Matt, you have completely changed my life. You're not going to believe what's happened."

Bobby had manifested almost a million dollars in just under a month, far exceeding the two hundred fifty thousand he initially sought. The story becomes even more incredible when he reveals that the sources of investment were completely unexpected; they came out of nowhere. He received recommendations from current investors and generous contributions from friends and family, and unexpected places and situations were approaching him. And there was Bobby, in a state of pure wonderment. In just one month, his company had transitioned from near collapse to the unexpected problem of too much interest, with his lawyers putting on the brakes, saying no more equity could be handed out.

I was no longer speaking with Bobby, trapped in fear and doubt; I was talking with Super Bobby. He had made the leap from wanting to being. He had not only manifested the funds needed to save his company but also transformed his entire being to align with his desires.

We all can find a bit of ourselves in Bobby's journey. Those moments of doubt, the anxious breaths before a decision, the weight of the unknown—we've all been there, in some shape or form, in our own lives. But look at Bobby. He overcame those hard times and came out on top.

By embodying his Super Bobby persona, he shifted his energy from lack to abundance, aligning his thoughts, emotions, and actions with the reality he desired to create. This transformation wasn't just about manifesting the funds he needed; it was about becoming the person he needed to be to attract that reality. By consistently showing up as Super Bobby, he sent a clear signal to the Universe that he was ready to receive the abundance he sought, and that reality collapsed into fruition.

In essence, what Bobby witnessed—and what you will discover—is that the key to unlocking true manifestation lies not in the pursuit of wanting but in the journey of being and consciously observing the reality you wish to create before it actually manifests. But this isn't just about reading this book and absorbing information; it's about putting these principles into practice. Just like Bobby, you'll need to create your own "Super Self"—the version of you that embodies the qualities, mindset, and energy of the person who has already manifested your desires.

To do this, you first need to understand who you are being currently and, more importantly, think about who you need to become. This is where the real work begins. It's time to take an honest look at your thoughts, beliefs, habits, and actions and ask yourself if they align with the person you need to be to manifest your desires.

PRACTICE:

Observing What You Lack

The purpose of this practice is to identify and acknowledge what you're missing in life. You will need either a journal, notepad and pen, or a notes app on your phone.

Step 1: Create Your Space
Find a quiet, private spot to be completely honest with yourself without interruption.

Step 2: Set Your Mindset
Take a deep breath. Remember, this exercise is about raw authenticity. There's no right or wrong—just honesty.

Step 3: List Your Wants
Write down everything you feel you lack or want. Be brutally honest. Don't censor yourself. Keep writing until you've exhausted all of your thoughts about what you're missing or what you desire.

Step 4: Feel It

After completing your list, sit with the surface emotions. How does seeing your wants and lacks laid bare make you feel? Write down these emotions.

Step 5: Dig Deeper

Reflect on these questions, and jot down your answers: How long have you carried these feelings of lack? What patterns do you notice in your wants and perceived shortcomings? How have these feelings of lack influenced your choices and actions?

Step 6: Acknowledge and Release

Take a deep breath. As you exhale, recognize that awareness is the first step to change. You're not trying to fix anything yet—you're simply shining a light on where you are.

This exercise isn't about solving your wants or addressing what you feel you lack. It's about facing your current reality head-on. Keep this inventory as you move through this book. It's the starting point for your journey from wanting to being.

It can be challenging to face the truth of who we are, especially when we're conditioned to believe certain things about ourselves and the world around us. So the real questions are: Who are you being? And who must you become to bridge the gap between your current reality and your desired future?

CHAPTER 3

Self-Observation

So much of our daily experience happens on unconscious autopilot. We move through life in a fog, missing the glaringly obvious, even when we believe we're paying attention. Psychologists Daniel Simons and Christopher Chabris, while working at Harvard University, conducted an experiment about attention that became a cornerstone in cognitive psychology. They filmed two groups, one wearing white shirts and the other wearing black, passing basketballs to each other around a circle. Participants were asked to count the number of passes made by the group in white shirts. As they focused on this task, a gorilla walked into the middle of the circle, faced the camera, thumped its chest, and walked away. Astonishingly, when questioned afterward, 50 percent of the participants admitted they had failed to notice the gorilla.

This wasn't a trick or an illusion; it demonstrated "inattentional blindness," which occurs when people fail to perceive an unexpected stimulus in plain sight. Their focus was so locked on counting passes that the obvious intrusion completely slipped by their consciousness.

Now, you might be thinking, "That's fascinating, but what does it have to do with manifestation?" Just like the participants in the gorilla experiment, we often go through our days with a narrow focus, our attention consumed by our goals, responsibilities, and the endless chatter of our minds. Our unconscious habits run the show, while we remain blissfully unaware of the thoughts, beliefs, and behaviors that subtly shape our reality. The result is that we become so preoccupied with counting basketball passes—our daily tasks and our responsibilities—we fail to notice the proverbial gorillas in our midst.

These unconscious patterns can take many forms:

- Self-limiting beliefs that hold you back
- Negative self-talk that erodes your confidence
- Unconscious behaviors that sabotage your progress

These "gorillas" slip by our awareness, and we lose the power to stop them. As a result, we are blind to the unseen forces that are subtly shaping our lives, even though they are right in front of us.

The Stimuli Overload

Our world is bustling with stimuli. From the moment we wake up to the final scroll through social media before bed, our minds are inundated with information, demands, and distractions. Emails flood our inboxes, messages ping from multiple apps, news headlines scream for our attention, and our to-do lists seem to grow longer by the minute.

With so much competing for our attention, it's no wonder we get swept up in the whirlwind of the external world and allow the gorillas to creep in when we're not looking. We become so entangled in the web of "must-do"s and "should-be"s that we fail to observe who we're being. Our vision narrows, focusing solely on the tasks we need to complete or the things we lack, often missing the broader spectrum of possibilities surrounding us.

I'm not suggesting you stop your digital lifestyle; I'm suggesting you try to become more grounded and present and start paying even more attention. As we've previously discussed, the foundation of manifestation is always in the present moment, and the Universe reflects your projection in the present.

So, if you're not paying attention, you will allow unconscious behaviors to run wild in the background, manifesting unwanted outcomes in your life. More importantly, as highlighted in chapter 1, observation collapses energy into matter on the subatomic level, which simply means your own observation—whether conscious or unconscious—is collapsing and manifesting outcomes in your life.

This realization should stop you in your tracks and make you question everything. How much of your life are you truly observing? Are you aware of the unconscious patterns and beliefs that are manifesting in your daily experience? Could it be that your unconscious observation is holding you back from creating the life you truly desire?

But here's the catch: you have a choice. You can take the blue pill, remain in the comfort of unconscious creation, and continue to manifest a reality that doesn't fully align with your true desires. The blue pill is seductive because it offers a sense of familiarity and security, allowing you to stay within the confines of your comfort zone and avoid confronting the deeper truths about yourself.

Or you can take the red pill—the path of self-observation, pure awareness, and conscious manifestation. This path requires courage and a willingness to confront the parts of yourself that you may have been avoiding. It means detaching from your ego—the persona you've crafted for the world—and diving deep into the essence of who you truly are. It's about becoming a witness to your own thoughts, emotions, and behaviors and asking yourself some tough questions along the way.

The Power of Self-Observation

Self-observation is the art of awareness. It's deliberately choosing to catch yourself when you are unconscious, running on autopilot, or triggered by external events. I like to approach this practice as a curious scientist, stepping back without judgment to study my own mind and behavior. It's about understanding why things are happening in a particular way. Initially, you're not trying to change or fix anything; you're simply observing what's there. It's about becoming a neutral witness to what's happening within and around you, without attachment or criticism. This may sound simple, but in our fast-paced, distraction-filled lives, it's a skill that requires practice and patience.

At times, this process can be uncomfortable. We're confronting the hidden corners of our personality that often go unnoticed. It's like shining a flashlight into the dark places of our psyche. It requires introspection—detaching from who you think you are to discover who you truly are. It takes willpower, sometimes a bruised ego, and an honest look in the mirror. Through this process, you will begin to understand yourself on a deeper level, and you'll start to see how your thoughts and emotions influence your actions and how your actions shape your reality. With this awareness, you can start to make conscious choices that ultimately align with the life you truly desire.

One of the key aspects of self-observation is nonjudgmental awareness. This means observing your inner experiences without labeling them as "good" or "bad," "right" or "wrong." It's about accepting what is, rather than immediately resisting or trying to change it. I'm not asking you to alter who you are or pretend to be a new person; I'm inviting you to simply start observing yourself to ensure that your actions and thoughts are aligned with who you aspire to become, and to identify any unconscious patterns that may be holding you back. When we judge ourselves, we create inner tension and conflict, which only generate negative and low vibrations. But when we observe with compassion and curiosity, we create space for understanding, growth, healing, and transformation, which creates a higher vibration that is more likely to be aligned with your vision.

Self-observation is the exact tool to help you with this alignment. It begins by initially turning your gaze away from what you want to manifest and redirecting it inward. I experienced the power of self-observation firsthand a year before I quit my corporate job. At the time, I was struggling with a lot of stress and felt as though a vice was clamped around my chest, making it difficult to breathe. I'm sure you can relate to the feeling of having too much on your plate. Then, from the least expected source, my wife's grandmother intervened. Her friend was a reflexologist—a specialist who practices an alternative therapy that works through applying pressure to specific points on the feet that correspond to different areas of the body and energy systems. She arranged for me to have a session at her house. Despite my vague understanding of what it involved, her insistence and my desperation for relief made me try it. As I lay back on the recliner, preparing myself for what I thought would be a simple foot massage, the therapist looked at me and asked a simple question: "So, Matt, tell me: Who are you?"

Automatically and with pride, I responded: "I'm twenty-six years old, an estate agent, and the youngest manager in my firm."

His gaze never wavered. "No, Matt, I didn't ask what you did for a living. I asked who you are."

It was a gut punch. Beyond the suit, the job title, and the relentless daily grind, who was I? Who was the person hidden behind the corporate shell? At that moment, I had an awakening. The distinction between "doing" and "being" was unveiled before me. Like the participants in the famous gorilla experiment, I had been so engrossed in counting the basketball passes of my life—the titles, achievements, and routines—I had failed to see the "real" me. I didn't know how to answer the question. Who is the person behind the suit? It was like stepping outside my body, seeing a thick shell, and trying to peek inside. What I thought was reflexology turned into one of the most significant realizations in my life: "Who am I?"

At that moment, I realized how completely I had lost myself in my corporate identity. The title, the achievement of being the youngest manager—these weren't who I was; they were just roles I played. They had become chains, constraining me to a version of myself that looked successful on paper but felt hollow inside. Whether intentional or not, that simple question was transformative. It made me see how easy it is to mistake what we do for who we are. And isn't that the most insidious form of blindness—when we're oblivious to our own essence? We become the titles we wear, the routines we follow, and the achievements we chase.

I had become so fixated on the tangible, on what could be measured and displayed, that I had lost sight of the intangible, the essence of who I truly was. All it took was a simple yet profound question during a reflexology session to shatter that illusion. I realized that a realm of untapped potential, desires, and dreams existed beneath the layers of corporate expectations.

As I lay there, I felt a shift occurring within me. It was as if the layers of my corporate persona were slowly peeling away, revealing a deeper, more authentic self that had been hidden. In that moment of stillness and reflection, I began to detach from the identity of Matt the real estate agent—the person who was always negative, complaining, fearful, and judging others—to suddenly finding the real me. The "I" in all of this. The consciousness; the witness; the awareness; the observer of my life. I was seeing myself clearly for the first time. I felt a sense of freedom and lightness. It was as if I had been wearing heavy iron armor that finally had been removed, exposing the vulnerable, authentic person inside. In just a few minutes, my whole perspective changed. I no longer saw myself as a real estate agent; in fact, I realized how much I hated it. For the first time, I found the guts to be real with myself and own up to what I truly wanted.

In the days and weeks that followed, all I did was observe. I couldn't believe how powerful it was to simply detach from my thoughts. I started to notice how often little things at work would wind me up: the constant moaning, the negative self-talk, and the deep feeling of being unfulfilled.

As I continued to observe my thoughts and feelings, I was gobsmacked to discover how much I'd been complaining and struggling in my job, all while pretending to enjoy it. I'd been so caught up in playing the role that was expected of me that I'd lost sight of my true self. This realization prompted a need for change—to set Corisande and myself free from the rat race. It became my initial want. But manifesting this dream required some proper soul-searching.

Who was the real Matt underneath all the layers? Why was he putting up with so much stress? What did freedom mean to him?

To manifest what we truly want, we've got to know ourselves inside out—beyond the titles and jobs—to our very core. Deep down, the real me had always wanted to help people and make a difference in the world. But I'd become so tangled up in expectations and conditioning that I'd buried this essential part of myself.

The truth is, you don't need a reflexology session to experience this kind of self-observation and awareness. All you need is the willingness to create a bit of space in your life, to slow down and be present with yourself. It's in these moments of stillness and reflection that you can begin to witness your thoughts, emotions, and behaviors with a bit of clarity and compassion.

So how do you start? There are many ways to practice self-observation, but here are five ways that I have found powerful in my manifestation journey:

P—Pay attention to your thoughts.

O—Observe and journal your findings.

W—Welcome honest feedback from your nearest and dearest.

E—Embrace the present moment.

R—Reframe limiting thoughts.

Pay Attention to Your Thoughts

In a 2014 study published in the journal *Science*, participants were asked to sit alone in a room for between six and fifteen minutes without any distractions, such as a smartphone, book, or pen and paper. They were simply asked to sit and entertain themselves with their own thoughts. During the study, participants were also given the option to administer a mild electric shock to themselves by pressing a button.

The researchers found that many participants struggled to sit alone with their thoughts, and some even preferred to administer the electric shock to themselves rather than sit in silence. Across eleven studies, 67 percent of men and 25 percent of women chose to shock themselves at least once during the thinking period. The study suggested that people have difficulty engaging with their own thoughts and that many prefer to engage in external stimulation, even if those activities are unpleasant, rather than be alone with their thoughts.

This study left me with several questions. What if, by paying attention to your thoughts, you realize that you are separate from them? What if, instead of feeling the need to escape or be distracted from your own mind, like the participants in this study, you could simply observe without attachment and discomfort? For instance, in your own life, are you aware of the constant chatter in your mind—the voice that comments on everything, judges every situation, and criticizes every decision? Have you ever paused to consider who is the one listening to that voice? If you are aware of it, does it mean something inside you is also observing it at the same time?

To illustrate this, let's try a simple exercise:

1. Close your eyes and silently repeat your name in your mind five times.
2. Then say it another five times, shouting as loudly as you can inside your mind.
3. Now, open your eyes.

Did you "hear" your name? Were you aware of an inner voice? Did it feel like you were a detached listener hearing your name, or did you perhaps visualize it? Maybe you saw your name in letters?

If so, who heard or saw it? You might answer, "Me." But who is this "Me"? You might then claim it was your name that heard it. But who is this "name"? Your name was the tag you were given at birth, not the one who heard it. You might then respond with "I." But who is this "I"?

At your core, you are pure consciousness, the ever-present observer, the awareness, the witness, the watcher—and that's who heard it. That's the part that I found during my reflexology session—the "I" who had always been there, buried from life.

This observer is always there, aware of your surroundings, thoughts, emotions, and even the label you know as your name. This name, an identity established at birth, doesn't encapsulate the entirety of your being. You are the observer, functioning above the surface of your thoughts.

Whatever you think you are not capable of, whatever anyone has said you can't do, realize it's just a thought—the awareness inside has the power to do and create anything it wants. This "I" is what you need to find inside; it wants to help you if you find the space to allow it to emerge.

Scientifically, this awareness of your thoughts is known as *metacognition*. The term comes from the word *meta*, meaning "beyond" or "on top of"—this simply means that you, as the observer, are always on top of your thoughts. Metacognition is the awareness of your thought processes and an understanding of the patterns behind them. It's like being in a movie theater, watching your thoughts play out on the screen while remaining separate from them. This ability is incredibly powerful, not just for manifestation but for every aspect of your life.

When you start observing your thoughts, you may notice

patterns and habits that no longer serve you. Maybe you find yourself worrying about the future or dwelling on past mistakes. By shining a light on these thought patterns, you can begin to change them. For example, imagine you're facing a challenging situation at work. By observing your thoughts, you might notice that you're engaging in negative self-talk, worrying about potential outcomes, or getting caught up in workplace gossip that drags you down emotionally. With this awareness, you can consciously choose to catch these thoughts and reframe them in a more positive light or simply allow them to pass by, like clouds in the sky, without attaching to them.

Or maybe you're dealing with financial stress, and you're reading this book to manifest more money. Without conscious observation, you might be constantly worrying about money, telling yourself and others that you're always broke, or thinking that money is impossible to come by. These thoughts can become so habitual that you don't even realize you're thinking them, and as a result, the thoughts lead to corresponding emotions, such as fear, anxiety, and stress. Often, these negative thoughts are first triggered by external factors, such as an unexpected bill, a comment from a family member, or even a social media post.

For instance, how many times have you been scrolling through Instagram and you see a friend away on a fancy vacation? Before you know it, a thought pops into your head: "I'll never be able to afford a vacation like that." That thought quickly spirals into feelings of envy, frustration, and hopelessness about your financial situation, and before you know it, one simple photo has ruined your entire day.

But with metacognition, you can catch that trigger, recognize the negative thought, and consciously reframe it to something like, "Wow, that vacation looks amazing! I'm so happy for them. I'd love to be away, but I trust my journey and know that the Universe will sort me out with my own dream vacation when the time's right."

I know this might seem difficult, and it is initially—we're so programmed to revert to self-blame and negativity that reframing a trigger and thought can be exhausting—but with enough practice, like any new habit, it starts to become automatic. This is important because the Universe will always give you what you are. So if you're always complaining about money, even if you consciously seek to manifest money, your programmed vibration is lack, which will only attract more wanting money. However, as you consciously observe, catch, reframe, and start cultivating more gratitude, you will attract circumstances on that emotional frequency, such as more money.

Observe and Journal Your Findings

Observing your thoughts and catching negative patterns is a skill that takes practice. One way to develop this metacognitive ability is through a simple self-observation exercise. By consciously tracking your thoughts, feelings, and reactions during a period of time and journaling your findings, you can gain valuable insights into your habitual patterns and the triggers that perpetuate them.

Journaling allows you to step back and observe your inner experience with curiosity and without judgment. As you bring awareness to your thoughts and emotions through writing, you'll naturally create more space between them and your true self, the observer. In that space lies the power to reframe limiting beliefs and align with the reality you wish to create.

Consider setting aside time each day to write down your observations. You might note your first thoughts upon waking, record any negative or self-limiting thoughts throughout the day, and reflect on patterns or recurring themes in the evening. Be honest with yourself, and record all thoughts without self-judgment. Over time, you'll begin to see the space between your true self and the thoughts that have been clouding your vision.

Welcome Honest Feedback from Your Nearest and Dearest

Sometimes, no matter how much we try to be aware of our own patterns and behaviors, there are blind spots that we just can't see. It's like trying to read the label when you're stuck inside the jar. The latest research tells us that by the age of thirty-five years old, 95 percent of our behaviors and habits are programmed subconsciously, so we might think we are aware of who we are being, but in reality, we're completely blind to it because those habits exist on autopilot beyond our conscious awareness.

How do we shine a light on these blind spots? That's where your nearest and dearest come in. They're the ones who see you, day in and day out, and notice all those little habits and quirks that might be holding you back from manifesting your dreams. They're aware of what you can't see, and their perspective and feedback are golden.

Now, I know asking for feedback can be tough, especially when it comes to our own shortcomings. But trust me, it's a game changer. When I was on my own manifestation journey, aiming to be recognized globally for helping people change their lives, I knew I needed an outside perspective. So I gathered my courage and sent a message to my closest friends and family. It went like this:

> Can you do me a favor? You know, we all have those little habits and behaviors that we might not even realize we have or are doing. Well, I want to know what mine are . . . I promise I won't take offense. Can you be honest with me about what you observe?
>
> Thanks, Matt

The responses I got were eye-opening. Here are a few:

- You don't always seem to be listening.
- A bit bossy and sometimes a bit hard.
- You are sometimes overorganized; try to step back and allow intuition to run through.
- You always make yourself busy.
- You sometimes get too serious about things.

Now, reading these responses wasn't exactly a walk in the park. It bruised my ego, and I felt uncomfortable, but it was exactly what I needed to know. If my dream was to help others, I wouldn't have gotten far without my wife pointing out that I was a bad listener!

So, let's bring this back to you. If you're looking to manifest love, for example, you've got to start by embodying love yourself. But how can you do that if you're not even aware of the ways you might be putting yourself down? If you're looking to manifest financial abundance, how can you do that if you don't even see how often you're complaining about money? That's where your loved ones' observations can be pure gold.

Here's my advice: find the strength and courage to try this exercise yourself. Choose three to five people who are closest to you, such as your spouse, children, parents, siblings, best friends, or colleagues at work. There's no right or wrong number; it's just got to be people you know will be honest with you.

When that feedback comes, remember to welcome it with an open mind and heart. This isn't about beating yourself up; it's about becoming aware of the patterns that might be holding you back so you can consciously work on shifting them.

Trust me, gathering outside perspectives is a crucial part of the manifestation journey. It takes courage, vulnerability, and a willingness to grow. But when you start aligning your energy and behaviors with what you want to attract, that's when the magic happens. Their feedback might offer you something you were completely blind to, and that itself might be the missing key you've been searching for all along.

Embrace the Present Moment

Once you've gained valuable insights from your nearest and dearest, and you're starting to observe your own thought patterns through journaling and self-reflection, it's time to bring your awareness to the present moment.

As we've discussed, the foundation of manifestation is always rooted in the present. The Universe is constantly responding to the energy you're broadcasting right now. So if you want to manifest your dreams, the most important thing you can do is to become more mindful of who you're being in this very moment.

I know it's easy to get caught up in the chaos of daily life. We're all guilty of dwelling on the past, worrying about the future, or getting lost in our thoughts. But the truth is, even when our minds are time-traveling, we're still here, in the present. That's why the feedback from our loved ones is so valuable. It helps us snap out of our mental chatter and see ourselves more clearly. When my wife told me I wasn't a great listener, it was a great wake-up call. I started catching myself in the act, noticing how often I'd mentally drift off during conversations. And that awareness was the first step to changing my behavior.

So, as you start implementing the insights from your loved ones, make it a priority to engage with the present moment as much as possible. Whether you're at work, spending time with family, or running errands, take a few seconds here and there to pause and check in with yourself. Ask yourself: "Am I fully present right now? Am I giving my complete attention to what I'm doing, or am I just going through the motions? Can I let go of my mental distractions and be here, fully and completely?" I know it's not always easy, especially when life is hectic. But remember, presence is a practice. It's about progress, not perfection.

Start small. Take a deep breath before answering a phone call. Really listen to your colleague during a meeting without planning your response. Savor your morning coffee, engaging all your senses with each sip.

In his book *Think Like a Monk*, Jay Shetty shares how the monks taught him to "drink his food and chew his water." Now, this wasn't meant literally; it was a metaphor for slowing down and being more present. When you eat, take the time to really absorb the flavors and nutrients as if you were drinking the food. And when you drink water, appreciate it, almost like you're chewing it. These simple exercises can help you become more mindful of what you're putting into your body and bring you back to the present moment. Try it for yourself today. At your next meal, slow down and really experience your food. Notice the colors, aromas, and textures. Chew each bite thoroughly, savoring the flavors. When you take a sip of water, pause for a moment to appreciate its coolness, its clarity.

Even these simple practices can significantly enhance your awareness of the present moment. And as you start bringing more presence into these basic activities, you'll find it easier to be present in other areas of your life, too. You can even make it a game. Set an alarm on your phone to check in with the present moment a few times throughout the day. Notice what you're seeing, hearing, feeling, and thinking. If your mind starts to wander, gently guide it back to the present.

Choose one activity today for which you'll be fully present, whether it's eating a meal, having a conversation, or taking a walk. Notice how it feels to be fully engaged, without distractions or mental chatter. Then, build from there, gradually expanding your presence practice into other areas of your life.

These might seem like small actions, but they're powerful. The more you can be present, the more you're aligning with the energy of the Universe. And when you're in alignment, that's when manifestation truly unfolds. By placing your full attention on whatever you're doing, you're mastering the art of being in the now—and that's the key to creating the life you've always dreamed of.

Reframe Limiting Thoughts

In life, we all face challenges, setbacks, and situations that can easily trigger a negative mindset. It's completely normal and part of the human experience. Our brains are wired to focus on potential threats and worst-case scenarios, which can lead us down a spiral of limiting beliefs and self-doubt. However, we have an incredible superpower at our disposal: the ability to reframe our perspectives.

Reframing involves consciously shifting how you view a situation or experience. Instead of dwelling on negative thoughts, you flip the script to a more positive, empowering perspective. The first step is to catch yourself when a limiting belief pops up and ask, "Is this thought serving me?" If not, it's time to reframe. One simple technique is to find the opposite of the negative thought. For instance, if your brain says, "I'm not good enough," reframe it as "I'm becoming better every day." It initially may feel forced, but with practice, it'll start to sink in.

Another helpful approach is to add a word like *yet*, which opens up possibilities. "I don't have the skills to start my own business" becomes "I don't have the skills yet, but I'm learning each day." That single word creates room for growth and progress.

Our thoughts shape our reality in subtle yet powerful ways. When we buy into negative, limiting beliefs, we act as if they're true. But when we reframe, we open ourselves up to new opportunities and possibilities.

To highlight the power of reframing, let's look at some common thoughts and how they can be transformed:

Common Negative Thought	Word Addition	Reframed Statement
"I don't have the resources."	Yet	"I don't have the resources yet, but I can get creative and find ways to make it work."
"I hate going for a run."	Get to	"I get to go for a run."
"What if I fail?"	Also	"What if I fail but also grow and learn valuable lessons?"
"This feels like such a risk."	Release	"I release fear and know that each step is guided by the Universe."
"Will I ever meet anyone?"	Trust	"I trust that I will meet someone when the time is right."
"I feel so fat."	Grateful	"I'm so grateful to have a body."

Common Negative Thought	Word Addition	Reframed Statement
"I hate myself."	Learning	"I'm learning to treat myself with compassion and kindness."
"I feel stressed."	And	"I feel stressed, and every day I'm taking steps to manage it."
"This isn't working."	Can	"This can work if I try another approach."
"Nothing is going my way."	Today	"Today might be tough, but every day brings new opportunities."
"I must sort this problem now."	Could	"I could take a moment to breathe and then tackle it."
"I have to do this."	Choose to	"I choose to do this because . . ."

Even with these reframing techniques, you may find yourself in situations where negative thoughts feel overpowering, and no matter how you try to reframe, you can't seem to shake them. This is when an "SOS reframe" can be a lifeline.

SOS reframing involves using short, powerful phrases to completely divert your mind from the negative spiral and bring you back to the present moment—back to your baseline awareness. These are mental reset buttons you can keep in your pocket for those moments when you're struggling to find a positive perspective.

Some go-to SOS reframes include the following:

- "I wonder what my next thought will be?" This stops the current thought loop by shifting your focus.
- "Is this FEAR [false evidence appearing real] talking?" Question whether the negativity is based on facts or fiction.
- "What am I grateful for in this moment?" Gratitude realigns you with a higher vibration.
- "Is this thought based on facts or feelings?" Separate objective reality from emotional reasoning.

The beauty of "I wonder what my next thought will be?" is that it breaks the negative thought pattern. We cannot dwell on two thoughts at once. This prompts your mind to let go and move forward openly, which is why I absolutely love it and always recommend it.

Remember, the goal isn't to ignore difficulties or pretend everything is perfect. It's about empowering yourself with perspectives that support you and get you back on track. Some days, a few small reframes may be enough. At other times, you'll need those bigger mental reset buttons.

Consistent practice is key. The more you reframe, the more naturally positive perspectives will arise. As your thought patterns shift, you'll experience positive ripples across your emotions, behaviors, and overall life experience.

PRACTICE:

Seven Days of Self-Observation

This exercise will help you cultivate the crucial habit of stepping back and observing your inner experience with curiosity and without judgment. When you become aware of your thoughts and feelings, you create distance between these temporary states and your essential self—the conscious observer. This separation gives you the freedom to transform restrictive thinking patterns and harmonize with your desired reality.

Purpose
To consciously train yourself to observe triggers, thoughts, feelings, and behavior.

Step 1: Gather Your Tools
A journal, a pen, and a phone.

Step 2: Morning Reflection
Immediately upon waking, note your first thoughts and feelings about the day ahead.

Step 3: Daytime Observations
Throughout the day, record negative or self-limiting thoughts and emotional reactions, especially those triggered by specific events.

Step 4: Evening Review
At night, transfer your notes to your journal. Look for patterns or recurring themes.

Step 5: Be Honest
Record all thoughts, positive or negative, without self-judgment.

Step 6: Weekly Review
At the end of the week, analyze your journal for insights. Understand how your thoughts shape your behavior and emotions, and consider what has triggered you the most.

Pro Tip
I learned from James Clear in his book *Atomic Habits* the power of "habit stacking." To ensure you don't forget this exercise, stack it with an existing habit like having lunch. For example: "When I eat lunch, I will jot down some observations from the day so far." Another could be: "Each time I make myself a cup of coffee/tea, I'll take a moment to check in with my thoughts and feelings and jot them down quickly."

Conclusion
This self-observation exercise is designed to help you uncover the root causes and triggers behind your negative thought patterns and limiting beliefs. By observing your inner world with curiosity and without judgment, you'll gain invaluable insights into the subconscious programs that have been shaping your reality. Over time, you'll begin to perceive the space between your true self and the thoughts that have been clouding your vision. In that space of awareness, you'll find the power to rewrite your mental scripts, release what no longer serves you, and align your thoughts and emotions with the life you truly desire to create.

Repeat this exercise as many times as needed until you feel you have a firm, conscious grip on your thought processes and the triggers that initiate them.

My goal in this chapter was to break down the importance of self-observation and prove to you that you have the power to consciously observe and, therefore, consciously create. We began by looking at how you are separate from your thoughts and, in the earlier chapters, how observation turns energy into matter.

Being the conscious observer, reframing is the crucial first step to manifestation. You can think positively all you want, but without this foundational ability to witness, question, and reframe your thoughts, you'll remain stuck in loops of negativity and limitation. With this vital first stage mastered, and now that you have a firm grip on self-observation, it's time to work on creating your intention for the future.

CHAPTER 4

Your Vision

In the 1960s, a young girl named Mae Jemison grew up watching the Apollo missions on TV but was often left feeling upset after not seeing any female astronauts. However, Jemison was so inspired by seeing actress Nichelle Nichols, who played Lieutenant Uhura on the TV show *Star Trek*, that she had a vision: to become an astronaut and one day travel to space. This was a bold vision, especially for a young Black girl, but with a love of science and a big dream, she was determined to make it happen.

Jemison's path was marked by determination and perseverance. After graduating from Stanford University and Cornell Medical School, she joined the Peace Corps, serving as a medical officer in Africa. But her true calling always remained space exploration. When Sally Ride became the first American woman in space in 1983, Jemison knew it was time to pursue her dream. She applied to NASA's astronaut program in 1985 but faced a heart-breaking setback when the program was put on hold. Despite the roadblock, she persevered and applied again. In 1987, she was eventually chosen as one of just fifteen candidates out of more than two thousand applicants, becoming the first Black woman admitted into NASA's astronaut training program. To put this into perspective, her selection represented less than a 1 percent chance of success. Most people would have had serious doubts in the face of a 99 percent probability of rejection, but not Jemison. Her unwavering faith in her vision propelled her forward.

After years of relentless dedication and rigorous training, in 1992, Mae Jemison's lifelong dream finally took flight. She blasted off on the Space Shuttle *Endeavour* and became the first Black woman in space. Amazingly, Mae's journey came full circle when actor LeVar Burton asked her to appear on an episode of *Star Trek*. Jemison agreed, becoming the first real astronaut featured on the show that had inspired her as a child. This incredible synchronicity highlights the power of holding a clear vision and trusting in the journey, regardless of the ups and downs.

Jemison's story perfectly encapsulates the essence of true manifestation. It reminds us that as long as we stay true to our vision and align with our intentions, especially in the face of setbacks and challenges, the right opportunities and synchronicities eventually will present themselves. When we do this, the stars align in our favor—sometimes quite literally, as in Jemison's incredible story.

As Jemison herself said, "Never limit yourself because of others' limited imagination; never limit others because of your own limited imagination." When it comes to your own vision, regardless of how big or bold it might seem, your job is to follow her lead and cultivate unshakable self-belief, feel the emotions of your desired future, and take inspired action, no matter how daunting the path may seem. When you stay true to your vision and keep moving forward, even when faced with uncertainty or challenges, the Universe will always have your back.

What Do You Want?

As we've explored, wanting plays a crucial role in the manifestation process. It's the spark that ignites our desire for change and sets us on the path toward creating a new reality. However, as you've learned in previous chapters, there's a paradox at play. While wanting is necessary to identify what we wish to manifest, dwelling too much on the absence of what we want can reinforce a sense of lack and attract more lack into our lives. So how do you navigate this paradox in relation to your vision? The key is to use wanting as a starting point and immediately move beyond it using the tools you will learn in this chapter.

At the end of chapter 2, you practiced listing everything you lack and want. It's now crucial to start shifting out of lack and into a new state that aligns with your future self. This means thinking, feeling, and acting as if your manifestation has already come to fruition. As you'll learn, you will do this by aligning your present state with the essence of your future self, using all the tools I use, such as visualization, meditation, journaling, gratitude, affirmations, and more. I like to call this keeping the gap closed between who you are and who you want to be; in a sense, as you close the gap, you stay aligned with the essence of your future and you avoid being caught up in lack. By closing the gap, you will begin to attract experiences, opportunities, synchronicities, and resources that align with the future you are seeking to manifest.

Now let me back up for a moment to clarify something important about manifestation. Many people get confused about setting a clear vision for the future. They think manifestation is just dreaming or putting images on a vision board and then waiting for them to magically appear. But that's not the whole picture. True manifestation involves cocreation, or working in partnership with the Universe. It's not about sitting back and waiting for the Universe to deliver your desires; it's about aligning your energy with the energy of the Universe and taking aligned, inspired action toward your vision.

I like to think of it as a dance. You take one step forward and allow the Universe to move with you. As you align your energy with the energy of your desires, the Universe responds by bringing opportunities that match your vibration. Take Jemison, for example; when NASA put the program on hold, she continued moving forward, held tight to her dream, and applied again. In a sense, the Universe was just one step behind.

Note that wanting in the vision stage is extremely important. As much as this book highlights the bigger problem with wanting, it's essential for getting clear on your vision. In fact, as you might expect, a common starting point for many people when they begin their manifestation journey is simply asking themselves, "What do I want?" This is a valid place to start when getting clear on your vision, yet too many people get stuck in this wanting phase. From my experience and working with people from around the world, I've observed that by asking the question, "What do I want?" you're often immediately thinking of external things that you believe will solve your internal problems. But how do you move forward? By asking a broad question, you avoid the steps necessary to cocreate and get into energetic alignment.

For example, you might say, "I want financial security," and the reason behind this desire is that you hope that when you manifest more money, something inside you will feel secure. Or perhaps you might say, "I want to meet my soulmate," and behind this desire is the hope that once you meet them, you'll feel love inside. However, these external desires highlight the lack you're currently embodying and don't help change who you are internally. As a result, you'll continue to live in lack and manifest more lack into your life.

Let me offer you a different perspective: whatever you think you want, it's not actually about that specific thing or person. When you express a desire, what's really happening is that you're seeing a version of yourself in your imagination who already has that desire fulfilled. Take manifesting a specific person, for example. It's not about that person; it's about the version of yourself you envision when you're with them: someone who feels deeply loved, at peace, at home. You're attracted to that future version of yourself, not the external specifics. This is crucial because it allows you to focus on becoming that version of yourself rather than fixating on the external want. And here's the beautiful irony: when you focus on becoming that version of yourself, you either collapse exactly what you thought you wanted into reality or something even better manifests, which you couldn't have consciously imagined.

So, how do we access this future version of ourselves? In my experience, having a specific timeline helps create clarity. Whenever I personally manifest, I think about a twelve-month version of myself who is already living the life I seek to manifest. Once I'm clear on who this version of me is, I break down the details and immediately start to embody him, moving beyond wanting. When I do this, I then let go of time, and in every case, everything I set to manifest in twelve months comes to fruition much sooner. It's important not to get too hung up on time because, as you've read, time itself doesn't exist; only the present moment does. However, a timeline aids with clarity of vision.

Whenever I think about the future version of myself who's already living my manifestation, I like to imagine that an infinite number of Matts exist in the future. You may recall from chapter 2 that I did this with my client Bobby. I asked him to visualize and clarify his Super Bobby persona. So I ask myself, "If there is a Super Matt out there, who do I want to be?"

Be-Do-Have

The Be-Do-Have coaching model is a powerful paradigm shift in how we approach goals and personal development. Most people believe they need to have something first, like money or success, before they can do certain things and be who they want to be. But this model flips that thinking: it teaches that we must first choose who we want to be, which then determines what we do, which ultimately creates what we have. I've discovered that this reverse approach is incredibly effective for manifestation. In fact, among all the methods for getting to a clear vision, this exercise has undoubtedly helped me and my clients the most.

What sets apart the Be-Do-Have approach is its ability to bridge the gap between vision and manifestation by providing a clear action plan. It guides you to move beyond wanting and into embodying your future self. The exercise asks you to consider not just what you want to have (your manifestations) but also who you need to become (your personality) and what you need to do (your actions and habits) to cocreate and make your vision a reality. In my practice, I've slightly tweaked the traditional Be-Do-Have questions to better suit the manifestation process, as originally presented by Stephen Covey in his influential work on personal effectiveness, *The 7 Habits of Highly Effective People*.

I love to contemplate the idea that an infinite number of future versions of me exist, and I ask myself, "Which one do I want to be?" Let me further unpack this concept to make it more tangible and then I'll invite you to try it out yourself. The "Be" aspect focuses on embodying your future self's traits, mindsets, and energy—the version of you that has already manifested your desires. It's about asking, "Who do I want to be?"

The "Do" component is particularly powerful, identifying the aligned actions and habits that will move you closer to your manifestations. It asks, "What did my future self do to become this person and live this life?"

The "Have" piece brings your vision to life by clarifying the tangible and intangible results of embodying your future self and taking aligned action. It's about asking, "What does my future self now have due to being this person?"

What I find so transformative about the Be-Do-Have approach is that it shifts you from a state of wanting to a state of being. Instead of waiting for a distant future, you start assuming the state of your future self in the present moment, living as if your manifestations are already a reality. You adopt your future self's mindset, habits, and behaviors, closing the energetic gap between where you are and where you want to be.

As you begin to embody this new state of being, the Universe cannot help but respond. Opportunities start appearing, synchronicities and serendipities unfold, and your external reality shifts to match your internal state. It's incredible. You become a vibrational match for your desires, and manifestation becomes a natural, effortless process.

And it all starts with a simple yet profound question: "Who do I want to be?"

How I Use Be-Do-Have to Get Clear on My Vision

In January 2023, I had fewer than a thousand Instagram followers and a big manifestation: to become a globally recognized manifestation coach, start writing a book, land a traditional publishing deal with a major publisher, and move to Cornwall in the UK to live by the sea. At the time, I couldn't help but wonder: "Could I make this happen? Could I be noticed in this crowded space? What did I need to do differently to reach the people who needed my message the most?" Although my analytical mind questioned, deep down, with all my years studying the science of manifestation, I knew this dream was already a reality. All I had to do was map it out, get clear, and align myself with my future self's energy.

The following are my Be-Do-Have notes to show you how I made it happen.

Be: In Twelve Months, Who Do I Want to Be?

I want to be a globally recognized manifestation coach, who positively influences hundreds of thousands of lives daily, and also an inspirational figure, giving practical, simple-to-understand, to-the-point advice, tips, and resources on how everyday people can use manifestation to create their best lives. I am an even better husband, more present, fun, spontaneous, and able to balance my love for work with an incredible life. I am living what I teach, trusting deeply in the unknown and the Universe. I master manifestation profoundly, continuing to research, learn, and deepen my spiritual practice. I make empowered choices about my health, fitness, and well-being. I live a life of freedom and joy, having moved to Cornwall to be by the sea, creating content with the ocean as my backdrop. I have a magnetic presence on camera with an authentic style. I write daily, bringing my dream of publishing a book into reality with a consistent writing practice. I'm known as a coach who helps people through multiple channels—courses, meditations, emails, podcasts, and videos across all social media platforms—not just one-on-one sessions.

Do: What Did I Do to Become This Person?

I leaned into being Super Matt, behaving and thinking like him and putting myself out there as if I was already globally recognized. I concentrated on my path, not comparing myself to others, and stayed laser-focused on my goals. Corisande and I teamed up to form a business that leveraged our unique strengths. We invested in top-quality equipment and eye-catching, vibrant clothes to make our content stand out. I committed to showing up consistently on social media and posting valuable insights twice a day. We took a significant risk and moved to Cornwall, even though we felt like we needed more time to be ready. We followed the signs, decoded our dreams, and trusted in the unknown. This move allowed us to create inspiring, colorful content against stunning ocean views. Without fail, I stuck to my morning routine, held my vision firm through daily meditation and mental rehearsal, visualized my content reaching those who needed it most, and imagined lives transformed by my work. I continued learning, reading, and going deeper with my own spiritual practices, finding creative and unique ways to manifest and explore more of my passion for the mystical. More importantly, I invited in fear, got comfortable with being uncomfortable, embraced risk, trusted my intuition, and followed signs and symbols that helped me take massive, inspired action. Most importantly, I embodied the feelings of my desired future in the present moment, living each day with gratitude, freedom, joy, and abundance.

Have: What Do I Get to Have Because of Being This Person?

I have a life that exceeds my wildest dreams, and I wake up each day with a sense of purpose, gratitude, and awe. I have the ultimate life, living with Corisande in Cornwall. We have a beautiful home where I can walk on the beach, feel inspired, and create content that uplifts others. I balance my work and personal life by coaching a few days per week, creating captivating content on the beach, and embracing the beauty of Cornwall in our spare time. Our business has exploded with growth, with a global community of more than two hundred fifty thousand people for whom my work resonates and who are manifesting their best lives. I have an engaged email list of ten thousand subscribers who look forward to my weekly newsletter insights. I have a transformative online course that helps people worldwide manifest miracles, and I have a series of guided meditations that help people connect with their future selves daily. I now have an incredible mentor who has opened their kind heart to share their wisdom on writing. I also have a brilliant New York–based literary agent who believes in my message and is passionate about bringing my work to the world. More importantly, my dream has come true: I have a publishing deal, allowing me to share my book with a broad audience around the globe.

After completing the Be-Do-Have exercise, I like to break down each question into different categories to really understand and integrate my vision. This method lets me look at my intentions from various angles and put together a practical road map for manifestation.

Here's my main intention and ultimate vision for the next twelve months: "To become globally recognized in the field of manifestation and secure a publishing deal."

This goal is my overarching target. I think of the main intention as the cake—it's ready, looks great, and is waiting to be enjoyed. But you can't have the cake without first getting the ingredients. These ingredients are the smaller steps or sub-intentions that come together to complete the whole. Think of manifestation as making the cake—if you don't have the recipe, you're just looking at the cake, which can be overwhelming.

To achieve this vision, I've mapped out the key sub-intentions, or ingredients, for my journey:

1. Post on social media twice a day to grow our business.
2. Develop a strong and authentic presence on camera.
3. Create and share courses, meditations, email newsletters, and engaging content.
4. Focus on health and fitness to get into the best shape of my life.
5. Expand my global following to more than two hundred fifty thousand people.
6. Find an incredible mentor and friend for guidance.
7. Secure a top New York literary agent.
8. Get a traditional publishing deal.
9. Move to Cornwall and start living our best life.

As I sit here a year later in my beautiful home office in Cornwall, reflecting on the Be-Do-Have exercise I started last year, I'm struck by how everything unfolded. Every intention I set has manifested, often surpassing my expectations. I've built a global community far beyond what I initially imagined. It's been a remarkable journey seeing my content resonate so deeply, with daily messages from individuals whose lives have been transformed by my work.

One of the most profound manifestations was meeting my mentor and friend, David—a truly brilliant and kindhearted man. David approached me in February 2023, a month after I did this exercise. Initially, we collaborated on a project and then out of the blue, he encouraged me to write a book. David was previously an American film producer, studio executive, and writer known for his work in major, award-winning films. Meeting someone of his caliber seemed beyond my wildest dreams. His mentorship is proof of the magic that unfolds when you truly believe in and commit to your path.

David is a big reason why you're reading this book. He helped me refine my voice and vision and introduced me to Steve, a New York literary agent with decades of experience. Steve, who shares my passion for manifestation, immediately connected with my message. I've always felt drawn to New York—I proposed to Corisande there, in Central Park—and having an agent based in the city seemed like a part of my destiny.

With Steve's help, I secured my biggest dream: a publishing deal with Penguin Random House, specifically with its Tarcher imprint in New York. It's almost humorous to think back on how, fifteen years ago, my English teacher doubted my writing skills, yet here I am, an author with one of the largest publishers in the world.

Why Manifesting Smaller Steps Works Like Magic

As you've just seen, I get clear on the overall picture—the cake—and then break it down into subcategories, or the smaller aspects of that manifestation. This approach helps me understand what I need to do next and keeps me in alignment with my ultimate manifestation.

Here's why this method is so powerful: When you focus on smaller, more immediate steps, they naturally feel closer and more achievable. This closeness makes it easier to believe in and align with each goal. This alignment is what accelerates the manifestation process, making each step unfold more quickly and effortlessly.

It's crucial to understand that these smaller manifestations aren't isolated successes. They're vital components of your bigger picture. Each step you manifest brings you closer to your bigger goal, keeping you energetically aligned and in harmony with your desires. This alignment is what makes the journey smoother and the goals more accessible. Without a doubt, this is the secret sauce of my own manifestation success.

Now, you might be wondering, "Isn't the whole point of manifestation to let the Universe figure it out?" Absolutely! And that's where the magic of this approach really shines. By breaking down your vision into smaller steps, you're not trying to control or manipulate the manifestation process. Instead, you're getting clearer on the next sequential step. We're still allowing the Universe to determine the how and when in perfect timing.

Think of it this way: it's easier to stay vibrationally aligned with a goal that feels within reach. When you're solely focused on a big, distant goal, it can create energetic disturbance. You might struggle to truly feel it as real. But when you focus on the next achievable step, it's easier to let go, to allow the Universe to step in and work its magic.

In my case, for example, manifesting a mentor was one of my sequential steps. I didn't force it to happen. I simply held the intention and remained open. And as you've read, that's exactly how David came into my life, perfectly aligning with my vision.

Remember, the smaller step is still manifesting the bigger goal. But because you can feel more aligned with it, the process unfolds more quickly. You're in harmony with it, dancing in step with the Universe.

So, as you move forward with your own manifestations, consider breaking them down into smaller, sequential steps. Get clear on what's next, align with it, and then let the Universe surprise and delight you with how it unfolds. That's when manifestation truly becomes magical.

Why Building a Vision Board Is Nonnegotiable

After completing the Be-Do-Have exercise and gaining clarity on all the elements that make up my vision, I love to take it a step further and create a vision board. This powerful tool has become integral to my manifestation process, and I want to share its importance with you. I'll admit I was initially skeptical about vision boards. They seemed too abstract for my taste, and I kept putting off creating one. But when I finally took the plunge and made my first vision board, I was amazed at the results. At the end of the year, everything I had put on that board had manifested in my life.

Imagine for a moment that you could take all those vivid images in your mind, all those powerful feelings of your future self, and bring them into the physical world. What if you could create a tangible representation of your dreams that you could see, touch, and connect with daily? This is the magic of a vision board.

When you create a vision board, you're taking the intangible—your thoughts, dreams, and desires—and giving them physical form. This act of creation is powerful, but it's just the beginning.

A vision board goes beyond representing what you want. It showcases the reality you have created and highlights all the elements that have come to fruition. Think of it as scrolling through your phone and looking at photos that represent your life. That's what we're aiming for here—a board that captures your life as if it's already happened.

When you look at your vision board, you activate your reticular activating system (RAS). Think of the RAS as your conscious mind's personal assistant, or gatekeeper, constantly filtering the massive amount of information you encounter daily. It decides what is important and what can be safely ignored. Therefore, regularly exposing yourself to your vision board tells your RAS, "This specific information is important. Pay attention to it."

Suddenly, you will start noticing opportunities and connections you might have overlooked before. It's like when you decide to buy a new car, and suddenly you see that particular model everywhere—your brain is now primed to recognize anything that could help you achieve your vision.

Your subconscious mind also plays a crucial role. It doesn't differentiate between what you've physically experienced and what you've vividly imagined. So with each viewing of your vision board, whether by active looking or in your peripheral vision, you're programming your subconscious to believe that this is your current reality. If you affirm on your board, "Money flows to me effortlessly," imagine how that will rewire any opposing beliefs in your subconscious. Over time, these new beliefs will shape your actions and decisions, often subconsciously aligning you more closely with your goals. I'll cover why this is so powerful in the next chapter.

A well-crafted vision board doesn't just show you what you want—it makes you feel it. When you look at images representing your future, you trigger a cascade of positive emotions. You start to feel the excitement, joy, and sense of accomplishment as if you've already achieved these goals. This emotional connection is the secret sauce of manifestation. It's about embodying the feeling of already having what you desire.

Creating Your Vision Board

When creating your vision board, there's no one-size-fits-all approach. The key is to choose a format that resonates with you and fits seamlessly into your daily life. I recommend using the ingredients that come up in your Be-Do-Have exercise. (You will do this at the end of this chapter.) Your board can be a collection of business, personal, health, wealth, and spiritual elements—whatever comes up for you during the next twelve months. Get it onto the board and make it real. To create my vision board, I use Canva, which is an excellent tool for this purpose.

Here are my five nonnegotiable tips for creating a compelling vision board:

1. Use the present tense: Frame everything on your board as if it has happened. This helps you embody the feeling of already having achieved your goals.
2. Make it visually appealing: Choose images and words that truly resonate with you. Your board should inspire and excite you every time you look at it.
3. Place it where you'll see it often: Put your vision board somewhere you'll see it multiple times a day. This could be on your bedroom wall, in your office, or even as a background on your digital devices.
4. Avoid past images: Don't use photos of yourself from the past. Remember, you're creating the future. Use images representing who you're becoming, not who you've been.
5. Use it as a meditation aid: I like to look at my vision board before meditation. It's beneficial for someone like me, who could be better at seeing in my mind's eye. Take a few moments each day to view your board and visualize yourself living that reality.

As you create your vision board, take your time. This isn't a race. It's about crafting a clear, compelling vision of your future. Be sure every element resonates with you deeply.

Don't shy away from specifics. Want a particular car model? Put it on there. Have a specific income goal? Write it down. Dreaming of a house with exact features? Find an image that matches, or sketch your ideal home if you can't find a photo. Think of your vision board as a GPS for your life. You wouldn't set out on a cross-country road trip with vague directions, would you? The same applies here. Give the Universe explicit, precise coordinates of where you want to go.

What works for me is taking my time to create the board and then embracing the concept of "set and forget." Once you've crafted your vision board, put it aside. Have it around you, but don't obsess over it. Things will manifest, some before others, and that's okay. Resist the temptation to change it constantly. I reflect and update my vision board each year, giving it time to work its magic.

Remember, manifestation is a journey. Sometimes, your vision may manifest slightly differently, and that's part of the process. Trust in the power of your vision board, and allow the Universe to work in its mysterious ways.

PRACTICE:

Be-Do-Have

In this practice, you will quiet your mind, ideally in a meditative state, and contemplate three simple yet powerful questions to gain clarity on your vision and align with your future self.

Preparation

Step 1: Create Your Environment

Find a quiet, comfortable place where you won't be disturbed for at least thirty minutes. This could be a corner of your bedroom, a peaceful spot in nature, or anywhere you feel at ease.

Step 2: Minimize Distractions

Remove any distractions, such as your phone, TV, or computer. This is your time to connect with your inner wisdom, so create an environment that supports introspection.

Step 3: Set the Atmosphere

To set the tone for your practice, you might light a candle, burn some incense, or play soft, soothing music.

Step 4: Prepare Your Tools

Have your journal and a pen ready to capture the insights that will flow.

Step 5: Center Yourself

Before you begin, take a few moments to center yourself. Close your eyes and take a few deep, slow breaths. Allow your body to relax and your mind to settle. You could do a short meditation to transition from your analytical mind to a more intuitive, receptive state.

Pro Tip

For the best experience, consider setting up your phone to record yourself so you won't feel distracted by remembering any insights. You can close your eyes and talk freely out loud. You can then journal insights afterward as you listen to the recording. This is how I like to do it.

Question 1: "In twelve months, who do I want to be?"

- While in this receptive state, start visualizing your future self—this version of you has already manifested your deepest desires.
- Allow your intuition to guide you. Write down your gut feelings and insights in your journal. Don't overthink it; allow yourself to channel whatever comes onto paper as you ask this question. You might get a sense of how this future self thinks and feels and what beliefs they hold.
- Let yourself explore how this future self interacts with others. Are they loving and kind, inspiring and uplifting? Do they have a way of making others feel seen, heard, and appreciated?
- As you connect with this future self, start to embody their energy. How does it feel to walk in their shoes? To see through their eyes?
- How do they carry themselves? What is their posture, their energy, their presence?

Question 2: "What did I do to become this person?"

- Imagine approaching your future self as your present self and asking them, "What did you do to become the person you are today? What actions did you take?"
- Let your intuition guide this dialogue. What do they say they did?

- You might ask what habits and routines they adopted and how they invested their time, energy, and money. Did they take any risks?
- Allow the conversation to flow naturally. Ask follow-up questions like, "How did you deal with the challenges and setbacks?"
- If it helps, try talking aloud with your eyes closed. The more curious and open you are in this dialogue, the more profound the insights will be.

Question 3: "What do I get to have because of being this person?"

- Visualize your future self walking you around their life. What do you see? Where are you living? Who are they with?
- Let them share freely. They might tell you about the tangible things they now have—a thriving business, financial abundance, a beautiful home, and vibrant health.
- They might share the incredible experiences they get to have—traveling the world, spending quality time with loved ones, and making a meaningful impact.
- Invite your future self to walk you through a typical day in their life. What do they do when they first wake up? How do they spend their time? Who do they interact with? How do they feel as they move through their day?
- How do they feel emotionally because they have this life?
- Let yourself fully imagine and feel this manifested reality. Engage all your senses. What do you see, hear, smell,

taste, and touch? The more vivid and immersive this experience, the more powerful it will be.

Integration and Next Steps

As you complete this practice, take a moment to sit with your insights. Notice how it feels in your body—the excitement, the joy, the gratitude. This feeling is a glimpse of your manifested reality. Take your time with this process. Revisit this experience as often as you need until each detail feels vivid and real. If visualization is challenging for you, don't worry. Many find it difficult to "see" with closed eyes. Try the exercise with your eyes open, relaxing and letting the insights flow as you journal.

Now, here's where the magic really begins. It's time to transform these powerful insights into a tangible representation of your future—your vision board. This is your crucial next step.

Go through your entries, and organize your insights into three key areas:

- Be: Your future self's personality traits, values, and mindset.
- Do: The actions, habits, and experiences that define their life.
- Have: The tangible and intangible results they've manifested.

These categories form the foundation of your vision board. As you create it, you're not just arranging images and words; you're constructing a blueprint of your future reality.

Throughout this book, we've been building toward this moment. True manifestation occurs when we align our entire being with our future self. By creating your vision board, you're taking a powerful step in that direction. You're not just dreaming; you're actively creating.

You'll notice a fundamental shift in your reality as you embody your future self's essence. People around you will see you showing up differently—tackling new challenges, radiating positivity, exuding new energy. The signal you broadcast to the Universe will change, attracting experiences aligned with your new state of being.

In the coming chapters, we'll explore powerful tools like meditation and visualization to strengthen your connection with your future self. But for now, focus on bringing your vision to life through your board. This is how you make your practice real, turning the vision of your future self into a tangible, visible guide.

As you continue this journey of embodying your future self, you may be confronted with limiting beliefs or doubts that try to pull you back into old patterns. You might start to observe thoughts or stories that try to convince you that your vision is out of reach or that you cannot achieve it. This is a natural part of the process, and it's important to remember that these beliefs do not reflect your true potential and what you are capable of manifesting.

These are the very beliefs we'll be working to transform in the next chapter, as we explore powerful techniques for reprogramming your mind to align with your vision.

CHAPTER 5

Believe

In 1979, a remarkable research program began at Princeton University that would challenge our understanding of the relationship between the human mind and the physical world. The study, led by Dr. Robert Jahn and his colleague Brenda Dunne, set out to investigate whether human consciousness, or "the observer," could directly influence the behavior of machines and electronic systems. This groundbreaking research, known as the Princeton Engineering Anomalies Research (PEAR) program, would span more than a decade and involve millions of trials, ultimately revealing the incredible power of the human mind and its ability to shape reality.

One of the most intriguing experiments conducted by the PEAR team involved random event generators (REGs), which are essentially electronic coin-flippers that produce random sequences of ones and zeros. Ordinary people from all walks of life were asked to sit in front of a REG and mentally will—or, in another sense, manifest—it to produce a more specific outcome, either more ones (which we can think of as "heads") or more zeros (or "tails"). The REGs were programmed to generate these outcomes with a 50/50 probability, just like flipping a coin. Statistically, over many trials, the REGs should have produced roughly equal numbers of ones and zeros.

But that's not what happened. Over twelve years and two and a half million trials, the PEAR team found that when participants focused their intention on producing more ones, the REGs began to behave in a way that defied statistical odds. The machines showed a small but persistent bias toward the intended outcome. The cumulative results of the PEAR experiments, as well as data from similar studies, strongly suggest that the human mind can interact with and influence physical reality at a fundamental level. The sheer volume of data and rigorous experiments make viewing these findings as coincidence or experimental error extremely difficult.

But here's where it gets really fascinating, and where we start to see the connection to manifestation. The researchers discovered that the participant's state of mind made a huge difference in their ability to influence the machine. Those who approached the task with a chilled-out, go-with-the-flow attitude; a sense of openness; curiosity; and what the researchers called *resonance* with the device tended to achieve better results.

On the flip side, those who got caught up in overthinking, analyzing, or doubting ended up sabotaging their own efforts. The more they tried to mentally force the outcome, the less influence they had on the REG. In fact, when the researchers asked the participants about their experiences, they found that the most successful ones were those who could get out of their own way and just accept that mind-machine interactions were a real thing.

Intrigued by these findings, I wondered if there were other experiments that could further cement the idea that one's state of mind can influence physical reality. What I discovered was both surprising and delightful—an experiment involving baby chicks that seems to perfectly illustrate the power of pure, uncluttered intention. French researcher René Peoc'h conducted an extraordinary experiment with newly hatched chicks. He imprinted the chicks on a small robot—essentially a mobile REG— as if it were their mother. The robot was programmed to move randomly within a circular arena, with its movements determined by a random number generator, much like the REGs in the PEAR experiments. When the robot was placed in the arena without the chicks present, it moved around randomly, as expected. But when the imprinted chicks were placed in a cage at the edge of the arena, something remarkable happened. The robot's movements became noticeably biased, spending significantly more time near the cage containing the chicks.

What makes this experiment so compelling in the context of our discussion on manifestation is the nature of the chicks' intention. These baby birds don't have complex subconscious beliefs or doubts. They haven't developed the mental chatter that so often sabotages our own manifestation efforts. Their intention is pure and singular: they simply want their "mother" (the robot) to be close to them, and they believe without question that this is possible.

In essence, these chicks are in a state of perfect coherence.

There's no conflict between their conscious desire and their subconscious beliefs. They're not in a state of lack or doubt; they're simply calling for what they believe should naturally be theirs. And in response to this pure, uncluttered intention, the physical world—in the form of the robot's movements—seems to bend to their will.

Now, let's pause for a moment and think about what this means for manifestation. How many times have you tried to manifest something in your life, only to find yourself overthinking and ultimately sabotaging your efforts? The PEAR experiments suggest that this mental chatter might be interfering with your ability to influence reality.

My own theory is that the subconscious mind and the belief systems we hold play a crucial role in our ability to manifest our intentions. Suppose someone has been conditioned to doubt their success due to past experiences or childhood programming; it is plausible that this could create more mental noise or interference when they attempt to influence reality. In other words, a person with deeply ingrained limiting beliefs might find it more challenging to achieve the relaxed, open-minded state that seems to influence the REGs or any other aspect of reality. Their subconscious doubts and insecurities could generate overthinking and mental chatter that disrupts the coherent signal needed for effective manifestation.

On the other hand, participants with more positive, self-affirming beliefs find it easier to get out of their own way and align their subconscious mind with their conscious desires, leading to better results in the PEAR experiments. And the baby chicks, with their pure and uncomplicated belief, demonstrate this principle perfectly. Deep-seated beliefs, often formed through early life experiences and programming, can either support or sabotage our conscious intentions, illustrating these underlying beliefs' significant but often unnoticed impact. Simply put, the formula needs to involve quieting this analytical chatter and aligning our deeper beliefs with our conscious intentions. By doing so, we can create a stronger, more harmonious signal to influence the world around us.

This is where the concept of coherence comes into play. Coherence is the state of being unified, balanced, and in harmony. When our thoughts, emotions, and beliefs are aligned, we create a clear and coherent signal that can influence the world around us. But when we doubt ourselves, overthink, or hold conflicting beliefs, we create internal conflict, which can cancel out our intentions and even sabotage our conscious desires.

Now, think about this in the context of your own life and what you're trying to manifest. If you can cultivate more peace, harmony, and coherence and adopt a more meditative, present mindset, you'll be sending out a clearer signal. Most people, however, are broadcasting a haphazard signal. For example, you might have all the conscious intent to find love, but subconsciously, you feel unworthy. Or you might be focused on attracting more money, but deep down, you feel broke and insecure. In these cases, you're sending out an incoherent signal, which can affect the outcome and even attract the opposite of what you want.

The data from the PEAR and baby chick experiments suggest that when your conscious mind is filled with doubt or overthinking, it cancels out your intentions or creates what's referred to as *incoherence*. It's like energy waves canceling each other out and not making a clear, focused signal. Returning to our radio analogy, it's like landing on a station but then slightly moving the dial until you're out of tune with the vibrational resonance. Remember, if 95 percent of who we are by age thirty-five is subconsciously programmed, then any subconscious belief that triggers conscious, analytical thoughts such as "I'm not good enough" or "I can't do this" has the potential to manifest the opposite of what you're seeking.

I named this chapter "Believe" because I want to emphasize the importance of believing in yourself, and the intentions that you seek to manifest, despite any subconscious beliefs that might be lurking within. In my own journey, as well as in the experiences of everyone I've worked with, I've noticed a pattern: when we hold subconscious limiting beliefs and don't observe and work on rewiring or changing them, and equally try to overanalyze, rationalize, doubt, or second-guess ourselves, or try to control how an outcome will manifest, it tends to take longer and in some cases might even result in the opposite of what we wanted. However, the good news is that, as the research proved, if you can align your belief system with your conscious intent, you will become more successful in manifesting material change.

Imagine if you could approach your own manifestation practices with the same purity of intention as those baby chicks. What if you could strip away any doubts, mental chatter, and ingrained limiting beliefs and simply hold your intentions with the same unwavering certainty? The results could be truly transformative.

Understanding Your Mind

Imagine for a moment that your mind is like a vast, unexplored ocean. The surface, with its choppy waves and constant motion, represents your conscious thoughts—the part of your mind that's always active, analyzing, planning, and worrying. But beneath this turbulent surface lies a calm, deep expanse—your subconscious mind. This is where the real magic of manifestation happens.

The PEAR experiments and the baby chick study we discussed earlier reveal that when it comes to influencing reality, what's happening beneath the surface matters more than the thoughts skimming across the top. Those participants who could quiet their analytical minds and tap into a deeper, more intuitive state could also bend reality to their will. And the baby chicks, with their pure, uncomplicated intention, showed us the power of belief uncluttered by doubt or overthinking.

So, what does this mean for your manifestation journey? You can have all the conscious intent in the world, crystal-clear goals, vivid vision boards, and perfectly crafted affirmations, but if your subconscious beliefs aren't aligned with these conscious desires, you're like a boat with its sail and rudder working against each other. You might move, but you'll struggle to reach your destination.

Your conscious mind is like the captain of a ship, making decisions and giving orders. But your subconscious? It's the vast, mighty ocean, with currents that can either propel your ship forward or hold it back. And just as the most skilled sailors learn to read and work with the ocean's currents, successful manifesters learn to align their conscious intentions with the deep currents of their subconscious beliefs.

The analytical part of your mind—the part that's always busy planning, critiquing, and problem-solving—operates in what neuroscientists call the "beta brain wave state." It's like the choppy surface of the ocean on a windy day. It's useful for navigating day-to-day life but not ideal for the kind of deep, transformative work required for powerful manifestation. To truly harness the power of your mind for manifestation, you need to dive beneath this turbulent surface into the calmer, deeper states. This is where you'll find the vast repository of your beliefs, memories, and learned behaviors—the currents that truly drive your life's journey.

But here's the challenge: while your conscious mind might be setting a course for abundance, success, or love, your subconscious might be running old programs of scarcity, unworthiness, or fear. It's like having a state-of-the-art GPS system guiding you toward your dream destination, but an old, outdated map ingrained in your ship's compass pulling you off course.

So, how do we align these two powerful forces? How do we ensure that the deep currents of our subconscious are flowing in the same direction as our conscious desires? This is where practices like meditation come into play. By regularly quieting the choppy surface of your mind, you can access these deeper states, reprogramming old beliefs and imprinting new ones that support your manifestation goals.

Remember how the PEAR study participants who could relax and go with the flow had better results? That's because they were tapping into these deeper brain wave states, aligning their entire being with their intention.

In my own journey, I've found that the moment I truly surrender to this process, letting go of the need to consciously control or force outcomes, something remarkable happens. It's as if the deep, powerful currents of my subconscious take over, effortlessly carrying me toward my desires. This is the state of coherence we talked about earlier—when your thoughts, emotions, and deepest beliefs are all aligned, creating a clear, powerful signal to the Universe.

As we move forward, we'll explore practical techniques to help you navigate these waters, aligning your conscious intent with your subconscious beliefs. Remember, the key to powerful manifestation isn't just setting clear goals or visualizing outcomes. It's in harmonizing the visible tip of the iceberg with the massive, hidden power beneath the surface. When you achieve this alignment, you'll manifest with an ease and power you never thought possible.

Brain Waves

To truly grasp the power of manifestation, we need to understand that a significant part of who we are is shaped by a deeprooted program, a set of unconscious behaviors and patterns learned through repeated experiences over the years. This programming primarily occurs during childhood and is heavily influenced by our brain wave states during these crucial years.

The adage "Give me a child until he is seven, and I will show you the man" isn't just an old saying; it's backed by neuroscience. On average, for the first seven years of life, the brain operates primarily in what's known as the *theta brain wave state*—a state similar to hypnosis. During this phase, children lack a fully developed analytical mind to question incoming information. Instead, they readily accept and surrender to information, absorbing it like a sponge. This is why children can easily believe in concepts like the Tooth Fairy or Santa Claus delivering presents worldwide in one night. During this theta-dominant phase, children are incredibly open to learning and absorbing information from their environment. They can pick up new languages easily, have unique creativity when playing and telling stories, and have a strong intuition. They're masters at being present and engaged in the current moment with a fluid, nonlinear way of thinking.

The beliefs, attitudes, and behaviors that children are exposed to during this time often set the blueprint for how they'll react and make choices later in life. To understand why this happens, let's talk about brain waves. Your brain consists of billions of neurons that communicate through electrical pulses. When you think, feel, or do anything, these neurons fire off signals. All of this activity creates brain waves, which look like wavy lines on a graph, kind of like ocean waves. These waves are measured in hertz (Hz), which tells us how many times the waves cycle per second.

There are five types of brain waves, including gamma, but for the purpose of our work, we'll focus on these four:

1. Beta waves (14–30 Hz): These waves dominate your
    waking day. Your consciousness or "observation" is
    focused on the outside material world. You use this
    state for mental tasks, problem-solving, and learning.

In this state, your conscious mind is in charge, making it tough to access your subconscious.

2. Alpha waves (8–13 Hz): These waves appear when you relax and meditate. When you daydream throughout the day, you float between beta (day) and alpha (dream) waves. In this state, your mind is open to suggestion and imagery, perfect for learning, being creative, and tapping into your subconscious.

3. Theta waves (4–7 Hz): These waves are linked to deep relaxation and the subconscious and are dominant during meditation and light sleep. This state is dreamlike and highly suggestible, like the brain wave state of young children.

4. Delta waves (0.5–3 Hz): These are the slowest brain waves associated with deep, dreamless sleep. In this state, the conscious mind is completely disengaged, and the subconscious is most accessible.

By purposely accessing the deeper alpha and theta brain wave states through practices like meditation, and even touching the deep delta state in some advanced practices, we can open a doorway to reshaping our subconscious landscape and aligning it with our conscious desires. This reprogramming process can be challenging. Our subconscious beliefs and patterns are deeply ingrained, not just in our minds but in our bodies, too. They often resist change because they're familiar and comfortable.

That's why understanding ourselves is crucial, as we discussed in chapter 3 on self-observation. We can spot the subconscious patterns holding us back by paying close attention to our thoughts, emotions, and physical sensations. Noticing how our bodies react to specific triggers and how our minds tend to worry or doubt in familiar ways is the first step in breaking free from unconscious living, where we're just reacting based on our past conditioning.

True manifestation isn't just about visualizing what we want; it's about aligning our entire being—mind, body, and spirit—with our vision. This means recognizing our limiting beliefs and patterns and having the courage and commitment to change them. As adults, we have the power to consciously observe our patterns and choose to reprogram ourselves. This might seem intimidating, but tools like meditation make the process easier. By quieting the analytical mind and slowing down our brain waves, we can access the subconscious, where we can replace limiting beliefs with empowering new ones that match our conscious intentions.

Meditate to Manifest

When I started out on my manifestation journey, I struggled to understand the connection between meditation and manifestation. In my mind, meditation was for those who could sit in the lotus position for hours on end—a practice that demanded a significant time commitment and unique set of skills. It felt out of reach for someone like me, who worked a nine-to-five corporate job and was just beginning to explore the world of personal growth and spirituality.

However, as I delved deeper into my journey, I discovered that through conscious visualization during meditation, I could tap into the power of my subconscious mind. By vividly imagining my desired manifestations, my deeper self began to believe that the manifestations were already happening. It was as if a switch had been flipped, and I could suddenly feel a strong emotional connection to my goals.

This was a huge turning point for me. The penny finally dropped, and I understood that manifestation wasn't about faking it until I made it. Instead, it was about genuinely embodying the energy and emotions of my desired reality. Meditation provided me with a sacred space to step into the version of myself who had already achieved my dreams and to feel the joy, gratitude, and fulfillment of a life full of abundance, financial security, travel, and freedom from my job.

Before this realization, I had struggled with the concept of "acting as if." How could I pretend that all my manifestations had already come to fruition when my current reality seemed so far from my goals? It felt inauthentic and even delusional at times. But as I grasped the true essence of meditation and its role in manifestation, everything began to fall into place.

The more I practiced, the sooner I could close my eyes, switch off from the outside world, and feel connected to my dreams. I became addicted. I'd bounce out of bed at 4:45 a.m., listen to a guided meditation, and mentally rehearse living the dream before leaving the house at 7 a.m. in my suit and tie to head to work. As I continued to practice, I found that my manifestations began to unfold in the physical world with a sense of ease and synchronicity that I had never experienced before. Opportunities aligned, and my external reality began to mirror the inner world I had been creating through my meditations.

With meditation, especially to manifest, the goal is to quiet the constant chatter of the conscious mind—the endless stream of thoughts, worries, and distractions that keep us stuck in the beta brain wave state—and transcend into the deeper state of our being. As you slow down and bypass the analytical mind, you gain access to your subconscious, where you become more receptive to new ideas and beliefs. When you are down in alpha, and even theta, the critical, analytical part of your mind that might normally reject affirmations or visualizations as "unrealistic" is quieted, allowing these new thoughts to take root in your subconscious.

In fact, when you slide down into the subconscious mind as the observer, you can start to visualize your future and align those deeper parts of yourself that are programmed differently. By doing this consistently, your conscious desires and subconscious beliefs move into alignment, and you send out a powerful, coherent signal that starts to influence your external reality. On the flip side, if you're too caught up in analytical thinking, you will create disturbance and noise, which can interfere with your manifestation.

Think of meditation as being a gardener planting a seed. Your conscious mind is like the topsoil—it's where you plant the seed of your intention. But for that seed to grow, it needs to penetrate deep into the rich soil of your subconscious. Meditation is the tool that allows you to dig past the surface level of your mind and plant your intentions deep in the fertile ground of your subconscious. To do this successfully, the first step is to identify and remove any weeds, rubble, or rocks that might hinder growth. This is like the self-observation process you learned in chapter 3, where you become aware of any limiting beliefs or blocks holding you back.

Here's how it works: As you meditate, focus on your breath, a mantra, or some form of guidance. This acts as an anchor, keeping your conscious mind occupied so you can slip into those deeper brain wave states. Once you're in a deep meditative state, you can begin to work with your subconscious. This is where techniques like visualization come in. By mentally rehearsing your desired reality in vivid detail (which we will cover in chapter 6), you start to impress these ideas onto your subconscious mind.

Remember, your subconscious mind and your body don't distinguish between what's real and vividly imagined. Think about how your body reacts to a nightmare—your heart races, you sweat, and it feels real for a moment. Now, imagine creating that power in reverse. When you visualize your desires in a deep meditative state, your body believes it's real and starts to think that you're living in that manifested landscape, making you feel equal to your future self, who is already living that life. So as you consistently hold these images and beliefs in your mind during meditation, your subconscious starts to accept them as true. It starts to align itself with your conscious intentions, and this is when manifestation begins to happen in your external reality.

With enough practice and presence, you can learn to go even deeper and reach the theta state. In these deeper states of mind, you can achieve a unique condition I like to call "conscious but asleep." Your body is in a state of deep relaxation, almost like sleep, but your consciousness—the observer within you—remains awake, and you are in the perfect environment for self-hypnosis, much like how children absorb information from their environment in their early years.

But your work doesn't end there. You must show up every day to tend to your garden, as a gardener would. You wouldn't plant seeds and then walk away. Instead, you'd make a daily practice of nurturing your seedlings. You'd water them, ensure they're getting enough sunlight, and protect them from weeds and pests. Similarly, in meditation, you show up each day to tend to your manifestations. You continue to visualize your desired future and feel the emotions of your dreams as if they've already come to fruition. And just as plants don't sprout overnight, your manifestations might not appear immediately. Persistence and patience are key.

Here's the beautiful part: just like a gardener isn't ultimately responsible for a seed blossoming into a flower, you aren't solely responsible for your desires manifesting in the physical world. There's a cocreative force at play, whether you call it the Universe, the Source, or Mother Nature. Your job is to set the intention, align your energy, and tend to your inner garden. The actual unfolding of your manifestation in the outer world is orchestrated by a power greater than yourself.

At first, your meditation practice might feel clunky or awkward, and that's completely normal. You're learning a new skill, and it takes time to develop. But with consistent practice, it will start to feel more natural. Eventually, quieting your mind and accessing your subconscious will become second nature, and you won't have to consciously think about each step.

This is powerful because when you get up from your meditation, you will no longer be feeling worried, stressed, anxious, envious, or sad. You will feel peace, love, compassion, happiness, and excitement. The more you practice accessing and maintaining these positive states through meditation, the more your state of being will become aligned with your future. That's when the synchronicities and opportunities start to show up, the outside world acts like a mirror reflecting your internal state, and your manifestations start to appear. The key is repetition. The more you practice, the more deeply ingrained the new beliefs become.

The Key to Rewiring Your Brain: Frequent Repetition

In a pioneering study, Dr. Phillippa Lally, a psychology researcher at University College London, published groundbreaking research on habit formation. Her team tracked ninety-six people for twelve weeks as they tried to make a new behavior, such as drinking water with lunch or running fifteen minutes before dinner, stick. On average, they found that it took more than two months for a new behavior to become fully automatic or habitual. However, there was a wide range, with some taking as little as eighteen days while others needing around 254 days for the new habit to solidify. This research underscores the power of frequent repetition, which is essentially a form of self-hypnosis. When you consistently repeat a thought, action, or way of being, you're gradually rewiring your brain and body to adopt it as the new normal. The sustained repetition slowly overrides your former habits and patterns, creating new neural pathways that support your desired behavior.

In the context of manifestation, this process is crucial. By repeatedly engaging in thoughts, behaviors, and emotional states aligned with your desired reality, you're not just wishing for change, you're actively rewiring your brain to support that change. This is where the concept of being rather than wanting comes into play.

As I've observed in my own manifestation practice, consistent repetition creates the most profound shifts. With enough repetition of visualizing and feeling yourself as your future self, you move beyond merely wanting something to being the person who already possesses it. You're no longer an observer dreaming about the future; you're actively embodying that future self in the present moment.

This process isn't always easy, especially in the first thirty days. It often feels unnatural at first, as you're challenging your brain's established neural pathways. You're up against your established program, routine, and automatic responses. Your body, accustomed to its current state, often resists change and may try to convince you that the new behavior is unnecessary or even harmful.

Let me illustrate this with a personal example. I recently committed to running five kilometers every morning as an experiment for this book. Initially, the idea of running in cold or rainy weather felt like a chore. I made the environment more appealing by investing in new running gear, but the initial excitement wore off quickly.

After about a week, my body started to rebel. I was used to finishing my meditation, making an espresso, and reading a book at seven a.m. Running disrupted this comfortable routine, and my mind produced every imaginable excuse: "You won't stick to this." "Running will do nothing for you." "What will the neighbors think?" Over the years, I've learned to observe such thoughts without getting caught up in them. Despite the resistance, I committed to the repetition. For the first few weeks, it was a daily struggle to get out the door. I was literally using the power of my mind to overcome my body's inertia. But I persisted, continually affirming, "I get to go for a run." Around the sixty-day mark, something shifted. Running had become less of an effort and more of an enjoyable routine. It felt as if my legs knew what to do without conscious intervention. As my body ran on autopilot, my mind was free to contemplate other things, like what I wanted to write that day. This experience aligns perfectly with Dr. Lally's research. It took about two months of consistent repetition for the new habit to become automatic, rewiring my brain and body in the process.

Consider your own life and what you're trying to manifest. It might seem daunting or challenging at first, and you might have numerous excuses for not starting. But what if your best life is just two months of consistent practice away?

If you dedicate yourself to frequently repeating thoughts, behaviors, and emotional states that align with your desired manifestation, you can expect to embody that new reality in about sixty-six days, on average. It simply takes consistent practice and patience to override the old, unconscious patterns. As you keep repeating and embodying your future self, the outer world will begin to reorganize around your new vibrational state, collapsing the potentiality of energy into the physical form through your new observation of reality.

PRACTICE:

The Sixty-Six-Day Accountability Challenge

It's time to take everything you've learned and put it into action with your own sixty-six-day manifestation accountability practice. This is where the real magic happens, where you shift from wanting your dreams to embodying and becoming them.

As you've just learned, science shows that it takes an average of sixty-six days for a new behavior to become automatic and habitual. When we apply this to manifestation, it means that by consistently practicing the habits and actions of your future self for sixty-six days straight, you're not just changing your behaviors; you're fundamentally reprogramming your subconscious identity to be that future person. By embodying the habits of your future self, you're not just visualizing or wanting the change; you're becoming the change on a deep, cellular level.

I can't stress enough how game-changing this practice is. Whether you're new to manifestation or you've been working with these principles for years, committing to this self-accountability will catalyze breakthroughs and shifts beyond what you've ever experienced. I've witnessed it countless times with my coaching clients and experienced the magic firsthand in my own life.

Here's how to get started:

Step 1: Identify Key Habits

Reflect on your Be-Do-Have exercise from chapter 4 and identify three to five key habits or actions that your future self consistently practices or does to be the person they are. These should be behaviors you can commit to doing every single day for the next sixty-six days. You can always start with a few core habits and build up from there as you gain momentum.

Step 2: Create a Tracking System

Create a visual tracker to keep yourself accountable and celebrate your progress. It can be as simple as a handwritten chart, or you can use a digital tracking app. Use green checkmarks for "done" and red x's for "missed"—the green represents that you are being your future, and the red represents the old you.

Note

If you're still working on the self-observation practice from chapter 3, where you observe and journal your thoughts, be sure to include that right away in your accountability. Once you complete the initial practice, if you continue it for another week, simply add it to your ongoing tracker.

Here's an example of what your initial tracker might include:

- Wake up at 5:30 a.m.
- Meditate
- Journal and observe thoughts
- Go to the gym
- Read ten pages of a book

When you hit a full week of green checkmarks on your tracker, treat yourself to a meaningful reward. This can be anything, but having a reward will help you stay motivated. If there is something that you plan on buying, save it for a full week of green checks and make it a game.

View your accountability journey as an evolving process—you'll grow and adapt over time. Feel free to continue certain practices until you intuitively feel it's time to modify or shift your approach. You will learn more tools throughout the rest of this book, which you can easily add to future weeks. Trust your intuition, and layer in any additional supportive practices that feel aligned for you.

Make the habit-building process more accessible by using proven techniques like habit stacking (anchoring your new habit to an existing one), optimizing your environment (like setting reminders or creating a dedicated space for your practice), and finding accountability partners (such as a friend who's also committed to their growth).

As you start your sixty-six-day journey, remember that you're rewiring your subconscious mind. Initially, it's normal for your old patterns and conditioning to resist the change. But if you stick with it, you'll reach a tipping point at which the new habits will start to feel natural and automatic. That's when you know you've truly stepped into the identity of your future self.

And here's the best part: the breakthroughs and manifestations that unfold from this practice will blow your mind. When you fully embody the energy and habits of your future self, your external reality can't help but shift to match that frequency. Synchronicities, opportunities, and "coincidences" will start popping up everywhere, aligning you with your desires in the most unexpected ways.

CHAPTER 6

Rehearse

Before we move on to the next step, let me ask you a question: Based on the information you've read so far in this book, do you now believe that your thoughts have some form of an impact on your external world? If you do, then you'll likely agree that you shouldn't miss a day rehearsing your future. If you're still not convinced because you need to see it to believe it, then this question is even more crucial for you. If you want to start seeing the life you dream of show up in your reality, then trust me, you can't skip a single day of rehearsal.

Rehearsal simply means visualization. It's about taking the images and scenes of the life you want and practicing them repeatedly in your mind as if you are already living that manifested reality. As mentioned in the last chapter, I do this through guided meditation to get beyond the busy chatter in my analytical mind. However, as you'll soon discover, there are several other effective ways to practice rehearsing your future, even if you have trouble "seeing images" in your mind's eye.

I used to struggle with visualization. Growing up, I didn't know how to play imaginatively; I always remember looking at my younger brother, James, lost in his mind while playing with a toy car, and I just didn't get it; I had to take the car apart to find fun. Even a few years ago, when I would try to mentally rehearse the life I was trying to manifest, I would just see darkness. It was frustrating initially, but with enough practice, I began to master it. My wife, Corisande, on the other hand, is an exceptional visualizer. She can close her eyes and be fully immersed in the scene; she's in a full-blown mind movie, experiencing the people, environment, colors, textures, sounds, and smells. Regardless of your current visualization abilities—whether you see vividly, don't see at all, or can't quiet your mind—there are tools to help you.

One of the most extraordinary examples of the power of mental rehearsal comes from a fascinating study done by researchers at the Cleveland Clinic Foundation. They wanted to see if people could increase their muscle strength by imagining themselves exercising without moving a muscle. They divided thirty volunteers into four groups. The first group visualized exercising a muscle in their little finger, the second group visualized exercising their elbow, the third group actually did physical exercises for their little finger, and the fourth group didn't do any training at all—they were the control group.

After twelve weeks of this mental training, just fifteen minutes a day, five days a week, the group that visualized exercising their little finger increased their finger strength by a massive

35 percent. The group that visualized their elbow exercises boosted their strength by 13.5 percent. And the group that physically trained their finger saw a 53 percent increase in strength. Meanwhile, as expected, the control group showed no significant changes.

In simple terms, just by thinking about exercising, these people strengthened the brain signals that control their muscles, ultimately making them stronger without any actual movement. Take a moment to really think about that. People got stronger just by visualizing it, without lifting a finger. Their thoughts changed their physical strength. This raises an intriguing question: If this can be done with muscle mass, why couldn't it be done with weight loss, recovery from health conditions, and anything else? If that's not proof of the mind's power over matter, I don't know what is.

The Power of Mental Rehearsal

Mental rehearsal isn't limited to lab experiments; it's a technique also employed by some of the world's greatest athletes. Consider Michael Phelps, the most decorated Olympian of all time with an astounding twenty-eight medals, twenty-three of which are gold. Phelps's success wasn't solely the result of grueling physical training. Mental rehearsal played a crucial role in his journey to the top. From a young age, Phelps's coach, Bob Bowman, recognized the importance of mental preparation. He provided Phelps's mother with a book on progressive relaxation techniques, which she read to Michael every night before bed. These techniques helped Phelps learn to relax and clear his mind, setting the stage for effective visualization.

In an interview, Bowman explained, "Once you can put yourself in a relaxed state, then I tell them, it's like watching a movie. It's essentially what it is. Sometimes, it's like you're sitting in the stands watching yourself swim, and sometimes, it's like you're in the water swimming. . . . The key to visualization is it has to be very vivid. It has to be rehearsed many, many times. And it works because the brain cannot distinguish between something that's really vividly visualized and something that's real."

By the time Phelps stepped onto the starting block in the World Championships or Olympic Games, he had already swum each race hundreds of times in his mind. This mental preparation allowed him to shut out everything else and let his body go on autopilot, executing the race he had visualized so many times before.

This brings us back to what we discussed in chapter 5 about the importance of being in a meditative state for impactful visualization and manifestation. By using relaxation techniques to quiet his analytical mind, Phelps could access the deeper states of consciousness where visualization is most potent. But Phelps didn't just visualize the perfect race. He also prepared for potential setbacks. In a YouTube interview, he explained how he also prepared his mind for things going wrong. In his own words: "When I would visualize, it would be what you want it to be, and what you don't want it to be," he said. "So, it's like you're always ready for anything that comes your way. If I have a suit rip, that's fine; I need another suit, I put it on. Any small thing that could go wrong, I'm ready for it."

This practice paid off spectacularly. During the two-hundred-meter butterfly final at the 2008 Olympics, Phelps's goggles began to leak as soon as he hit the water. By the end of the first lap, his goggles had filled with water, and he was essentially swimming blind. But it didn't faze him. He'd visualized this scenario, and his brain and body knew exactly what to do. He reverted to his mental rehearsal and swam blind for the remaining one hundred seventy-five meters, winning gold and breaking the world record.

It's important to note that while manifestation often focuses on positive outcomes, mental rehearsal can be equally powerful for navigating challenges. You might be going through a difficult time—perhaps a breakup, tense family dynamics, or stressful work relationships. In these situations, mental rehearsal can help you overcome immediate hurdles. For instance, if you're in a job with high tension and negativity, your instinct might be to get swept up in the drama. But with mental rehearsal, you have another choice. You can visualize who you want to be in these moments, mentally practicing how you can observe instead of absorb negativity, respond to challenges, and maintain your energy, regardless of the chaos around you. Or perhaps you've recognized that small things trigger low-vibrational emotions like anger and frustration. These negative emotional responses can keep your dreams and desires on a different frequency, making them harder to manifest. But by visualizing how you're going to show up in the world each day, how you'll react to triggers, and how you'll stay in control of your emotions, you can train your body to vibrate at a higher frequency. You can align with the energy of your best self, the version of you that's already living your manifested dreams.

The more consistently and vividly you practice this mental rehearsal, the more naturally you'll embody these qualities in real life. You're not just making your present reality more manageable; you're paving the way for your larger manifestations to align and come to fruition more quickly and easily. This is because, as you consistently show up as your best self, you're rewiring your brain on a physical level. You're building new neural pathways that support your desired thoughts, emotions, and behaviors, making them your default mode of being.

Neuroplasticity

You've probably heard the saying "You can't teach an old dog new tricks," and you might be thinking that maybe you are "too old" or "not good enough" to manifest change. However, when it comes to your brain, this couldn't be further from the truth. Historically, scientists believed that the brain's structure was primarily fixed by adulthood. However, with advances in neuroscience, scientists have come to understand that our brains can change and adapt throughout our lives, a phenomenon called *neuroplasticity*.

Think of your brain as a network of pathways, similar to trails in a forest. Most of these trails are well-worn and regularly used, representing your habitual thoughts and behaviors. But just as in a real forest, you always have a choice. At any moment, you can decide to veer off the beaten path and create a new trail toward a new destination. Forging a new path isn't easy at first. It means navigating unfamiliar terrain and getting snagged by branches. It can be tiring and frustrating, and there's always the temptation to return to the comfort of well-trodden routes. This same concept plays out in your brain when you start mentally rehearsing a new future.

Let's say you've made the decision to start mentally rehearsing a new future, one that aligns with your deepest dreams and desires. At first, your brain is likely to resist. It will try to default to those familiar "known" pathways to save energy. The new pathways you're attempting to create through mental rehearsal are unfamiliar and require more effort. Your brain, always seeking efficiency, will naturally want to redirect you back to the well-worn paths of your current reality. These old patterns include your habitual thoughts and beliefs, that inner voice that says things like "I'm not good enough" or "This won't work." But as you now understand, you are the observer of these thoughts. You have the power to consciously redirect your mind, even when it feels challenging.

As you persist in your mental rehearsal, something extraordinary begins to happen in your brain. Neurons, the cells responsible for transmitting information, begin to spark and connect in new ways. Neuroscientists have a saying: "Neurons that fire together, wire together." This means that as you repeatedly imagine your future, you're building and strengthening new neural pathways. Just as a trail in the forest becomes more defined with each traveler, these new pathways in your brain become clearer and more established with each repetition of your mental rehearsal.

Your brain starts to treat your visualized future as a real, lived experience, forming neural clusters that resemble memory pathways.

In a sense, if a neuroscientist were to peek inside your brain after consistent mental rehearsal, they would see pathways indicating that the future you've been envisioning has already happened. Your brain is effectively "remembering" your future, even before it physically manifests.

Now, let's take a moment to really appreciate this. When your brain looks like your future has already happened due to frequent rehearsals, you're no longer wanting that future. Instead, you've moved beyond it. You have transitioned into being that future self inside your brain, embodying the thoughts, emotions, and beliefs of the person living your desired reality. This is where the magic of effortless manifestation comes in. As your brain becomes hardwired to align with your desired future, you'll find that opportunities, resources, and experiences that match your vision start to flow into your life with ease. What once felt like a struggle to manifest becomes a natural, almost automatic process.

Here's the truly exciting part: as you continue to engage in this process, especially as you transcend your analytical mind, you're effectively observing your future as if it's your current reality. And as you learned in chapter 1, observation has a profound impact on the physical world. You're collapsing quantum possibilities into tangible reality by consistently focusing your observation on your desired future.

Over time, with dedicated practice, these new neural pathways become your brain's preferred routes. Your mind starts to automatically gravitate toward thoughts and visions that align with your goals rather than defaulting to past limitations. You're rewiring yourself, on a fundamental level, to think, feel, and behave like the person who has already achieved your dreams.

How to Mentally Rehearse Your Future

When it comes to mentally rehearsing the future you seek to create, the key is to make it as vivid, detailed, and emotionally engaging as possible. Your goal is to create a mental film, a story that's so real your mind and body can't help but believe it's your current reality. You're becoming the writer, producer, director, and actor of your own life movie. This process should be fun and engaging, something you really look forward to doing. It's an opportunity to step away from your busy world and go within, to connect with your deepest desires and bring them to life in your imagination.

I love to do this during meditation because it helps me slow down my brain and find the present moment, which is the foundation for manifestation. When we're fully present, we're not caught up in the worries of the past or the anxieties of the future. We're in a state of openness and receptivity. To start, revisit your Be-Do-Have notes from chapter 4 and focus on what your future gets to have. The "Have" aspect represents the physical manifestations and emotions that your future self is living. One of the most powerful ways to create this narrative is to envision your perfect day in the future, where all your dreams and goals have already manifested. This is a day in the life of your future self, living in complete alignment with your desires.

It doesn't matter what you're seeking to manifest, whether it's launching a successful podcast, attracting the perfect partner, buying your dream house, starting a family, paying off debt, healing from a health condition, losing weight, feeling happier, traveling the world, or getting a scholarship. Whatever represents your primary manifestation, imagine a perfect future day where everything comes to fruition.

For broader or more complex manifestations like money, I suggest thinking about the flow of the money. Where is it going? What will you spend it on? If you're looking to manifest a specific amount, ask yourself why. It's always the energetic byproduct of money that you really want.

A common question is whether you can manifest multiple intentions at once. The simple answer is yes! However, if you're just starting out, focusing on attracting multiple things simultaneously might feel overwhelming. If that's the case, keep it simple. Focus on one or two main intentions and the sub-intentions that make up these desires. Sub-intentions are like the individual ingredients that make up your main desire. They're the smaller manifestations that contribute to the overall picture. For example, let's say you intend to manifest a successful podcast and quit your corporate job. Some sub-intentions might be these:

- I have built my dream podcast studio.
- I now earn enough from my podcast to quit my corporate job.
- I have ten thousand YouTube subscribers.
- Brand sponsorships and partnerships flow with ease.
- I attract inspirational guests who align with my niche.

Once you're clear on what your future self has manifested, it's time to flesh out the other aspects that will make up this perfect day. For the podcast example, consider elements like the following:

- Location: A well-equipped, professional studio designed for high-quality audio and video recording.
- People: Thought leaders, experts, and influencers who align with your podcast's niche.
- Daily activities: Brainstorming episodes, planning guest interviews, engaging with your audience on social media, creating promotional content, and analyzing metrics.
- Emotions: Feeling the joy of seeing your podcast grow, appreciation for the support from listeners and sponsors, inspired by guests, relief from leaving a stressful job, and the freedom to design your days and have more time with family.
- Purpose: Raising collective awareness, creating a supportive community, and inspiring listeners to make positive changes in their lives.

As you craft this detailed vision, it's important to engage all five senses, not just your sense of sight. Your mental rehearsal becomes most powerful when it engages every aspect of sensory experience—what you see, hear, smell, taste, and feel. The same goes for your mental rehearsal practice. The more senses you can involve in your visualization, the more real it will feel to your subconscious mind.

For example, let's say part of your perfect day involves a morning walk on the beach. Don't just visualize the scene; really step into the full experience. Feel the sand beneath your feet and the warmth of the sun on your skin, hear the crash of the waves, see the boats bobbing on the waves, smell the salty air, and taste the ocean mist. The more vivid and multisensory you can make these details, the more your brain will respond as if it's a real experience. You're not just creating a mental image; you're creating a fully immersive mental reality. You're tricking your brain into believing that your desired future is already a reality. The more convincing you can make this "trick" through multisensory visualization, the more readily your brain will accept and adapt to this new reality.

So as you map out your vision, whether it's for your perfect day or a specific goal, really take the time to engage all of your senses. What specific sights, sounds, smells, tastes, and physical sensations would be present in this desired reality? The more detailed and sensory-rich you can make your mental rehearsal, the more powerfully it will imprint on your subconscious mind.

Make Monday Great

Let me share a pivotal moment in my journey when my biggest dream was to manifest a life of freedom for Corisande and me—to quit our corporate jobs and start earning an income online. As I began thinking about my perfect day, I realized I could sum up the essence of this vision in just three words: *make Monday great*.

Why Monday? For most people in the corporate world,

Monday is often the worst day of the week. It's the day we drag ourselves back to the office, the day we're farthest from the freedom of the weekend. I thought to myself, "If time is just an illusion and all that exists is the present moment, why should I feel one way on a Saturday and the complete opposite way on a Monday?"

So I decided that as soon as I quit my corporate job, Monday would become the best day of the week. I planned out that day in meticulous detail, employing the visualization techniques we've discussed. I dreamed about what I'd do in the morning, picturing Corisande and I going out for breakfast at nine a.m.— exactly when I used to be stuck in high-pressure morning meetings.

We'd go for a beautiful walk late in the morning with our dogs, head into town for lunch and some shopping, buy something nice for dinner, and then head back home to cook together and enjoy a relaxing evening. It would be nothing fancy but something that meant the world to us. Especially on a Monday.

I rehearsed every aspect of this perfect day, using all five of my senses as much as I could. I could see us sitting in our favorite coffee shop, savoring our usual breakfast and sipping on flat whites, knowing that at nine a.m., everyone else was just starting their workday. I visualized the environment, the taste of breakfast, the sounds of people around us talking, and the feeling of holding Corisande's hand and imagining myself saying, "We've done it; we're free." This vision encapsulated the essence of the freedom I was seeking: the ability to design my days, be present with my wife, and enjoy life without being chained to a desk.

And let me tell you, when that perfect day finally came to

fruition, it was the best feeling in the world. Experiencing in real life what I had visualized so many times was a profound confirmation of the power of mental rehearsal and manifestation.

Here's the beautiful part: your perfect day doesn't happen just once. It can become a blueprint you return to repeatedly. In fact, to this very day, I never work on a Monday. All my clients know about this. I don't take calls; I don't book meetings; I don't do anything work related. Monday is sacred. It's the day I honor my younger self's dream and celebrate the freedom I've manifested. This is the power of your perfect day. It's not just a one-time event. It's a recurring celebration of your manifestation coming to life. It's a way to keep aligning yourself with the energy of your dream, to keep strengthening those neural pathways of abundance and joy.

And the more you mentally rehearse this day, the more real it becomes. Each time you slip into that meditation and visualize, you generate the feelings, the excitement, and the certainty that this is your future. You're mapping your brain to believe that this day has already happened and is your new normal. So when it does finally unfold in physical reality, it feels both incredible and somehow expected, and that's because you've lived it so many times in your mind. It feels a bit like welcoming an old friend.

Create Your Own Visualization Playlist

On our journey, Corisande and I have found that carefully curating a collection of songs that resonate with different aspects of our future has been one of the most powerful tools for getting into alignment, especially for me, as someone who doesn't always find it easy to "see" during visualization.

It's incredible how music has the ability to evoke emotions and transport us to different mental states. By intentionally selecting tracks that align with the feelings and scenes of your perfect day, you can create an immersive experience that anchors you in your desired reality. Here's the approach that's worked wonders for me:

Start by breaking down your perfect day into key scenes or segments. Then, search for music that complements each of these moments. I've found this to be one of the most effective ways to really tap into the emotions of my manifestation during meditation. I use Spotify, but feel free to use whichever platform you prefer. The length of your playlist will depend on your intended meditation duration. For a fifteen-minute session, you might choose four or five tracks; a thirty-minute immersion could include up to ten songs. The important thing is to ensure that each track represents a specific scene from your perfect day sequentially. You want the first track to represent the morning or first scene and then each following track gradually takes you through the day.

When choosing your songs, I recommend opting for music you enjoy but haven't yet attached strong memories to. This allows you to create fresh associations, linking the tracks to your future rather than your past. I'm a huge fan of Hans Zimmer for this purpose. His instrumental pieces allow me to fully immerse myself in my visualization. For instance, when I was manifesting our move to Cornwall and my vision of living freely by the beach, I used Zimmer's "Now We Are Free" from the *Gladiator* soundtrack. The emotions of the piece perfectly capture the feelings I wanted to embody as I pictured myself walking along the shore on our moving day.

As you curate your playlist, consider why each track resonates with your future self. Music can evoke specific emotional states, so choose songs that lift you into feelings of joy, love, abundance, freedom, or whatever your perfect day encapsulates.

If you prefer music with lyrics, go for it; just ensure they don't distract you from your vision. Keep in mind that the purpose of these songs is to anchor you to your future rather than re-mind you of past events. So take your time and be intentional with your selections.

Once you've crafted your playlist, give it a name that reflects your future, like "My Manifested Life" or "My Perfect Day."

PRACTICE:

Rehearse Your Future

By this point in the book, you should have a clear vision of what you seek to manifest, your perfect day mapped out, and your manifestation playlist ready to go. Now, it's time to bring it all together into a daily practice.

First, let's set up your ideal meditation environment. Find a comfortable spot where you can sit undisturbed, either on the floor or in a chair. If you're sitting on the floor, consider using a cushion or a mat to support your posture. If you opt for a chair, be sure your back is supported and your feet are firmly planted on the ground. I recommend not lying down, especially in bed, because you have already associated this position with sleep, which defeats the objective. The goal is for your body to be in a rested, sleeplike state while your consciousness remains awake.

To enhance your meditation experience, I highly recommend investing in a 100 percent blackout eye mask. This simple tool can make a world of difference by blocking out any distracting light and helping you achieve a more immersive state of relaxation. When you put on your eye mask, it's a signal to your mind that it's time to turn inward and disconnect from the external world.

When it comes to timing your practice, consistency is key. I find that meditating first thing in the morning or last thing at night tends to be most effective (as your brain waves are naturally slower during these times, making it easier to quiet the analytical mind), but what matters most is choosing a time that you can stick to daily.

Now, you have five options for your mental rehearsal. Try them sequentially during the next five days, in this order:

Step 1: Practice Guided Manifestation Meditation
If you're new to meditation or find it challenging to visualize on your own, guided meditation can be a fantastic starting point. I offer a variety of manifestation-focused meditations on my website, mattcooke.me, each designed to help you relax, connect with your vision, and impress your desires upon your subconscious mind. Simply find a comfortable position, put on your headphones, and allow my voice to guide you through the process.

Step 2: Listen to Your Visualization Playlist

Press play, close your eyes, and let each track guide you through a different scene of your perfect day. As the music shifts, allow your focus to flow from one moment to the next, fully immersing yourself in the sights, sounds, and sensations of your desired reality. Really feel the emotions of each scene, allowing the music to anchor you in the experience.

Step 3: Try Silent Practice

As you become more comfortable with the process of mental rehearsal, you may find that you're able to drop into the state of visualization more easily on your own. In this case, simply set a timer for your desired meditation length (I recommend starting with ten to fifteen minutes and gradually building up to longer sessions), close your eyes, and mentally walk through your perfect day or your specific manifestation scene. If you find it challenging to hold a clear visual image in your mind, try narrating the scene to yourself, either internally or out loud, describing each detail as if you were painting a picture with your words.

Step 4: Script Your Vision

For those who connect deeply with the written word, scripting can be a powerful manifestation tool. Put on your playlist, light a candle, and open your journal to a fresh page. Then, begin writing out your perfect day or your desired manifestation as if it's already happened. Let the music guide your words and emotions, and don't hold back. The more specific and sensory-rich your writing, the more deeply it will impress upon your subconscious mind.

Step 5: Go for a Walk or Run

Put on your headphones, start your playlist, and complement your movement with rehearsing your future. Your eyes don't always need to be closed. Go for a walk or run as if you are your future self, allow your playlist to guide you, and feel the energy in your body. Physiology is a great way to feel it. This is one of my favorite ways to rehearse my future.

Now, you might be wondering, "But won't moving my body keep my analytical mind active?" It's true that physical movement can keep us alert, but the key is to focus on the feeling of being your future self. When you immerse yourself in the emotional state of your desired reality, you naturally quiet your analytical mind and shift into a more intuitive, receptive state of being. So even though your body is in motion, your mind can still drop into the slower brain wave states that facilitate powerful visualization and manifestation.

It's important to remember that there is no one-size-fits-all approach to mental rehearsal. Depending on the practice you choose, you might find that you don't have enough time to visualize your entire perfect day in one sitting. That's completely okay! If you're short on time, focus on rehearsing a specific scene or moment that feels particularly charged with positive emotions. You can always revisit other parts of your perfect day in future practice sessions.

If creating a "perfect day" narrative doesn't resonate with you, that's fine, too. The key is to find a visualization style that feels authentic and inspiring to you. Whether you choose to mentally rehearse specific events, different manifestations, or a day in the life of your future self, the most important thing is to engage with your vision consistently and emotionally.

Commit to at least ten to thirty minutes per day to start with. If your mind wanders, gently bring it back to your vision. You'll find it easier to stay immersed in your desired reality with practice.

Remember, manifestation is a journey. You may find that your vision evolves as you continue to rehearse your perfect day. New details may emerge, or your priorities may shift. This is normal and a sign that you're growing and expanding. Allow your practice to evolve with you, updating your scenes, playlist, or guided meditations as needed. The beautiful thing about mental rehearsal is that it's not about rigidly clinging to a fixed outcome. It's about aligning with the feelings and essence of your desired life and allowing the Universe to bring it into form, often in ways you couldn't have initially imagined.

CHAPTER 7

Feel It Till You Make It

A year after selling our house and putting our worldly belongings in storage, Corisande and I found ourselves stuck. We'd moved in with her parents temporarily while we tried to manifest a house in Cornwall. We thought it would be a quick process—a few months at most—but despite our best efforts, we couldn't find a house that met our needs, and a year had slipped by. This was proving to be one of the toughest challenges I'd ever faced in manifestation, and the more frustrated I became, the more distant Cornwall seemed.

It was a paradox I was aware of yet couldn't escape. We'd been trying so hard to manifest our ultimate dream of relocating to Cornwall, but the consequence of that intense focus was that we were caught up in the lack of it. We were so attached to the idea that it constantly reminded us of what we didn't have. I'm sure you can relate to this—when you want something so badly that it consumes your thoughts. But the more you focus on it, the more elusive it becomes. You end up feeling stuck, frustrated, and perhaps even a bit foolish for wanting it so much. It's as if the very intensity of your desire pushes your goal farther away, leaving you in a state of emotional turmoil. The irony was that I was teaching this exact point, that if you attach to a desired outcome, you emotionally vibrate the opposite, such as lack and frustration. It's one of the hardest things to do because the solution is letting go and trusting, yet it often feels like you're giving up.

With this in mind and no conscious way to predict our move, we bit the bullet, packed our car, left our life in storage, and just went to Cornwall. We had no proper plan, apart from three months of sporadic accommodation in yurts, campsites, Airbnbs, and a few vacation cottages. We planned to tour Cornwall to truly feel the place, and we were determined not to leave without a new home.

The first month was exhilarating—a proper adventure that freed our spirits. We embraced every moment, even finding joy in the unexpected, like the few nights we camped in the back of our car when our tent started to leak. These experiences became some of the happiest times of our lives. Thankfully, my digital marketing business was doing well enough to support this nomadic lifestyle, allowing us to immerse ourselves in the journey without financial worries. But after a month, everything changed.

At the time, my focus on manifestation was purely value-based, and I was not making an income from it. It was a hobby, and at the same time, I was wrestling with a professional dilemma. Half of me was enjoying our nomadic life, enjoying posting manifestation content on social media, while the other half was falling out of love with digital marketing. It was clear that my passion lay not in launching campaigns, but in helping people change their lives through manifestation. This realization caused tensions with my business partner, and our paths began to diverge.

I had to make a tough call. Closing my marketing business was a risky move because it was the primary source of income for Corisande and me and key to our move to Cornwall. But at the same time, the emotional state it was creating within me wasn't in harmony with someone who would be able to manifest a dream house and life in Cornwall.

This crossroads brought me to one of my lowest points. Despite knowing so much about manifestation, yet having worked so hard for years to grow an income online after leaving our corporate jobs, could I risk it all again? I'd been here before, without a clue how we'd make it work, but the Universe had our backs. Why would it be any different this time?

This internal struggle is a common experience on the manifestation journey. It's what psychologists call "cognitive dissonance"—the mental discomfort that results from holding two conflicting beliefs, values, or attitudes. In my case, it was the conflict between my knowledge of manifestation principles and my fear of financial instability.

So I took another chance with the unknown. With very supportive in-laws, we made the hard choice to move back in with Corisande's parents in Shropshire. After three months in Cornwall, it was time to regroup and go back to the drawing board. I shut down the marketing business, separated from my business partner, and decided to pour 100 percent of my energy into my true calling: manifestation.

As expected, the naysayers piped up. "What happened to Cornwall?" "No longer moving?" "Maybe it was just wishful thinking to try moving to Cornwall." If you're wondering why Cornwall is so special to us, and why people doubted we would make it happen, imagine a place adored not just by its residents but also by about five million tourists each year, making it one of the UK's top holiday destinations. Cornwall has rugged coastlines, historic towns, and beaches serene enough to rival those of the Maldives. For Corisande and me, there's no other place on Earth that beats it. Here, the fight for sea-view properties is intense; landing a spot in Cornwall is a bit like snagging a rare gem—highly sought after and often challenging.

For the next twelve months, we parked Cornwall to one side, knowing that letting go of it was not giving up; it was getting us into alignment. We put our heads down and together started focusing entirely on building our manifestation coaching business. Although Shropshire was quiet and nothing like the vibrant coastal life of Cornwall, we committed to embodying the feelings of the life we wanted: freedom, fun, adventure, peace, happiness, and excitement. We never stopped envisioning our life in Cornwall. I mentally rehearsed it daily in meditation, seeing our life in my mind's eye, and I refused to get up until my body felt it emotionally. I would then get out of meditation and make a conscious effort to hold on to the feelings throughout the day.

Our time in Cornwall taught us something crucial. It helped us understand how living in Cornwall felt, which was invaluable. More importantly, it revealed the true essence of manifestation: the power of feeling. We realized that the key wasn't just in wanting or visualizing our dream, but in embodying the emotions associated with it. The secret was to feel those emotions—the freedom, excitement, and peace we associated with Cornwall—before the physical manifestation occurred. By opening our hearts and immersing ourselves in these feelings, we were turning our state of lack into a state of having.

This emotional alignment was crucial. It wasn't about pretending we already lived in Cornwall, but about capturing and living the essence of what Cornwall represented to us. By doing so, we moved beyond wanting and into vibrational harmony with our desire. We were no longer reaching for something outside ourselves, but cultivating those feelings within, regardless of our physical location. This shift in perspective and emotional state was the bridge that would ultimately lead us from wanting to having, from dreaming to manifesting. It was our gateway to aligning with the frequency of our desired reality.

Within six months, we grew our Instagram account to more than one hundred thousand followers and threw ourselves into our new venture. My coaching business started to explode, and at the same time, despite living in a sleepy, rural part of England, we made it our mission to fall in love with our life. We found activities that made us feel the way we imagined we'd feel in Cornwall. We explored, had fun, found new dining spots, had days out, got excited about building something meaningful together, and even made a conscious effort to be more present with each other and took our health seriously, going on a huge health kick that left us feeling proud and energized.

Paradoxically, we found ourselves falling in love with where we were living. We recognized that this wasn't a betrayal of our Cornwall dream, but rather a step toward it. By appreciating and finding joy in our present circumstances, we were aligning ourselves energetically with the life we desired.

After another year of living with Corisande's parents, everything changed. We manifested the perfect house in Cornwall. The synchronicities and signs that led us to this home were nothing short of magical. (I'll delve into these incredible details in chapter 12.) It was a property that exceeded our expectations, checking every box and then some, and was situated in the perfect location.

The most incredible aspect of this manifestation was that we weren't actively searching for it. We knew a house would eventually come our way, but we weren't fixated on the when or how. We were too engrossed in living our best life right where we were. As we focused on the present moment and cultivated the emotional state we associated with our dream life in Cornwall, we aligned ourselves with the frequency of that reality, bringing it to fruition.

The lesson here is profound: you can't fake having something you don't, but you can tap into the emotions associated with your desires. When you align your current emotional state with the life you aspire to lead, you send a clear signal to the Universe. It's not about letting external circumstances define you, but about cultivating the internal emotional landscape that resonates with your dreams.

Once you achieve this emotional alignment with your aspirations, you transcend the state of wanting or lacking. Instead, you're living your dream life on an emotional level, and the physical manifestation becomes a natural progression—a reflection of the internal reality you've already created.

This journey taught us that manifestation isn't about constantly focusing on what you lack or desperately wanting something to change. It's about embodying the essence of your desires in the here and now, regardless of your current circumstances. It's about finding ways to feel the emotions of your dream life today, and not waiting for external conditions to change before you allow yourself to feel good.

In essence, the secret to powerful manifestation lies in your ability to close the gap between your current emotional state and the emotional state of your desired reality. When you can consistently feel as if your dreams have already come true, you create a magnetic force that draws those dreams into your physical reality.

Energy in Motion

Emotions are, at their core, energy in motion. It's evident in the word itself: *e-motion*. As this energy flows through us, it generates sensations we interpret as feelings. Consider the experience of excitement: when it courses through your body, your heart rate increases, your gestures become more animated, and your voice might even rise in pitch. This is energy in motion, creating a sensation of lightness or buoyancy.

On the flip side, when you're feeling down, you might notice a heaviness in your limbs, a slowing of your movements, and a dampening of your usual enthusiasm. Again, that's energy—just moving differently, creating sensations of weight or fatigue. Slower or denser emotional energy often makes us feel heavy, tired, or frustrated. It's like trying to run underwater. Higher-vibrational emotions, on the other hand, can make us feel light, energized, and free. It's the difference between trudging up a hill with a heavy backpack and soaring effortlessly through the air.

It's crucial to understand the subtle yet significant difference between emotions and feelings, terms often used interchangeably, although they're not quite the same. Emotions are universal responses to stimuli such as joy, anger, fear, and sadness. On the other hand, feelings are our unique, personal sensations of these emotions. Think about it like this: we all know what happiness is as an emotion, but how you feel when you're happy might differ from how I feel. You might experience a lightness in your chest, while I might feel a warmth spreading through my body. These are our individual feelings.

Understanding your emotions and feelings is paramount when it comes to manifestation. It's not just about identifying the emotions of your future self, but also truly tuning in to how those emotions manifest as physical sensations within you. This is the key to attracting and maintaining resonance with your desires. When visualizing your future, don't simply label the emotions you anticipate feeling. Delve deeply into the sensations in your body. For example: How does excitement feel to you specifically? Where do you feel it? Where is it located in your body? The more intimately you understand these personal feelings, the easier it becomes to recreate them in your daily life, keeping you aligned with your manifestation goals.

The Universe doesn't just respond to your thoughts; it's also tuned in to your energy, which is a cocktail of your emotions and unique feelings. When you master both, you're fine-tuning your ability to stay in vibrational sync with what you want. This is the big secret that most people miss when it comes to manifestation. They get crystal clear on their vision, sure, but they forget to cultivate the emotions that go hand in hand with that future. That mismatch is like trying to tune in to a radio station using the wrong frequency. It makes attracting what you want feel like an uphill battle.

Think about it. Whatever you're trying to manifest, whatever reason brought you to this book, it all boils down to how you want to feel. Once you have that thing in your life, you'll feel a certain way. So why wait? Why stick around in that wanting phase? The real secret to moving beyond want is to feel it now, in this moment.

Imagine you're ordering a meal at a restaurant. You don't just sit there, hungry and miserable, waiting for the food to arrive. You engage in conversation, enjoy the ambiance, and maybe sip a drink. You're already in the experience of dining out. Manifestation works the same way. You don't wait to feel good until your desire manifests; you start feeling good now.

I'm all about keeping things simple, so here's the deal: if you can feel the emotions of your future now, you'll be in alignment with that future. That's it. It's that simple. It's not your job to predict, control, fight, force, worry, or question the how and when of your desire coming to life. Your job is to feel it until you make it and consciously keep yourself in that sweet spot of alignment.

You might be wondering, "How do I know if I'm in alignment?" Don't look outside yourself for the answer—it's all about what's going on inside. Your emotions are like a compass, pointing to what you're attracting, so make it a habit to check in with yourself regularly. Are you feeling light, excited, and joyful? Or heavy, anxious, and doubtful? These feelings are your guidance system.

Let's say your goal is to launch your dream business. The emotions tied to that might be excitement, freedom, and a sense of purpose. By consciously tapping into these feelings, you're not just twiddling your thumbs, waiting to feel successful once you've hit your goal. Instead, you're creating an internal environment that aligns with your goal.

This process isn't always straightforward. There will be days when you falter, when doubts creep in. It's like learning to ride a bike—you'll wobble and maybe even fall a few times. In these moments, it's essential to recommit to your practice. Sit in meditation, focus on those feelings, and persist until your entire being resonates with the emotion of your future self. Like any skill, this emotional attunement improves with practice. With time and dedication, you'll develop the ability to shape your emotional state at will, effectively bridging the gap between where you are and what you want. It's a practice, and like any practice, it gets easier the more you do it.

Remember, you're not just waiting for your life to change; you're actively changing your life by changing how you feel.

Emotional Vibrational Chart

Not all emotions are equal when it comes to manifestation. Some vibrate at higher frequencies than others, making them more powerful attractors. Understanding this emotional hierarchy can be a game changer on your manifestation journey. It's like having a road map for your feelings, showing you exactly where you are and where you need to go to align with your desires.

Dr. David Hawkins, a psychiatrist and consciousness researcher, introduced the Map of Consciousness in his book *Power vs. Force*. This map assigns numerical values to different emotional states, helping us understand emotions as vibrations of energy. Hawkins used a method called *kinesiology*, or muscle testing, to measure these emotional frequencies. He would have a subject think of a particular emotion or concept while he applied pressure to their outstretched arm. The strength or weakness of the muscle response indicated the vibrational level of that emotion. His scale ranges from one to one thousand. Shame, for example, vibrates at around twenty, while love vibrates at five hundred. Love is widely recognized as a powerful vibration, often regarded as an energy that vibrates at 528 Hz, which refers to the number of wavelengths per second.

I like to think of emotion as energy that moves in waves, called *wavelengths*. Higher-vibrational emotions, such as love or joy, have a higher frequency, meaning the waves move faster and closer together. Visualize these as tightly packed, rapid waves with very little space between them. On the other hand, lower-vibrational emotions such as fear or anger have a lower frequency, resulting in slower, more spread-out waves with larger gaps between them.

According to Hawkins's work, lower-vibration emotions such as grief, guilt, sadness, frustration, fear, and anger vibrate at slower frequencies. This sluggish energy makes us feel denser and more physical rather than feeling light and energetic. We all can relate to times when we feel stressed or sad, our bodies feel heavy, and we have less energy to do anything. Conversely, when we feel "in the zone," we have the energy to run a marathon—that's the level of energy coursing through your body.

Hawkins explained that as we raise our level of consciousness (or awareness), toward the higher end of the scale, we evolve from forcing outcomes to having power. Now, stick with me here because true manifestation is not about forcing; it's about effortlessly having the power to consciously create. When we raise our level of emotional consciousness into power, cultivating emotions such as acceptance, reason, love, and peace, we get our power back. Let's say you want to manifest something specific. Think about how that desired outcome makes you feel. Does it uplift you and fill you with joy, peace, or love? If it does, then according to Hawkins's scale, your desire naturally resonates with those higher frequencies where manifestation is most powerful.

This made sense to me. While I could force an outcome, I also could surrender and work on my internal emotional dial. For example, falling in love with my life before I manifested our move to Cornwall was paradoxical but also the key to the manifestation.

Now, here's why this matters for manifestation: the closer together these emotional waves, the less distance energy has to travel, and the faster manifestation can occur. When you're in a high vibrational state, you're shortening the distance between you and your desires. It's like upgrading from a dial-up internet connection to fiber optic—your intentions can manifest at lightning speed.

Remember that we're always in a state of creation, whether

we're conscious of it or not. I'm not saying you can't manifest if you're feeling frustrated or angry, but your energy is moving slower, which is likely to delay your manifestation. Because energy creates matter, if we're creating from a unified field of energy, then revving up our emotional frequency to be more like energy than dense matter will, in my experience, make manifestations arrive quicker.

Let's consider an analogy that might hit home. Imagine you're trying to send a message across a vast ocean by creating ripples. If you're operating at a low frequency (like when you're feeling fear or lack), your ripples are far apart. Your message (or, in manifestation terms, your desire) takes ages to reach the other side, and it might lose strength along the way. But if you're operating at a high frequency (like when you're feeling love or gratitude), your ripples are close together. Your message travels faster and maintains its strength longer. It's similar to the difference between whispering your desires and shouting them from the rooftops.

This is why people often find themselves stuck in a state of wanting or lack. They're operating at lower frequencies, creating wider gaps between their energy waves and making the manifestation process feel arduous. It's exhausting and seemingly neverending. To transcend this wanting paradox and truly get beyond wanting, we need to crank up the speed of our emotional state. By elevating our emotions, we're closing the energetic gap between us and our desires. We're creating an express lane for manifestation to occur.

Below is a simplified version of my emotional vibrational chart, inspired by the ground-breaking work of Dr. Hawkins and the revolutionary insights of Dr. Joe Dispenza, who brilliantly explains how emotions impact reality in his book *Becoming Supernatural*. This chart has become the cornerstone of my practice and is a powerful tool for transformation.

The Emotional Vibrational Scale from Wanting to Being: Journey of Manifestation

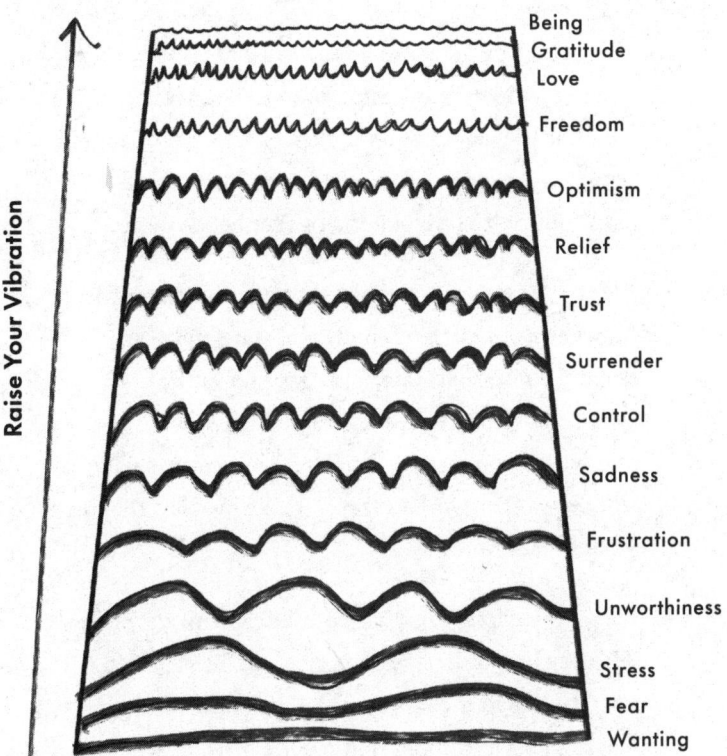

Lower vibrations, such as fear, create resistance and distance from your desires, while higher vibrations, such as gratitude, align you with the flow of manifestation, shortening the gap between you and what you seek.

Here's how you can use this chart effectively:

1. **Reflect on your current emotional state:** How does your life make you feel right now? Be honest with yourself. You might feel frustrated, worried, anxious, sad, hurt, desperate, or lonely. Mark these emotions on the lower end of the scale.

2. **Visualize your desired emotions:** Think about what you're trying to manifest. How will you feel once you've achieved it? You might feel love, peace, relief, happiness, excitement, or freedom. Mark these emotions on the higher end of the scale.

3. **Identify the emotional gap:** Look at the distance between your current emotional state and your desired emotional state. This gap shows the vibrational difference between where you are now and where you want to be. This gap explains why simply wanting something often keeps you stuck in a state of lack.

4. **Close the gap by moving your energy up the scale:** The key to manifestation is closing this gap. You need to lift your current emotional state to match the higher-vibrational frequencies of your desired emotions. When you do this, you create a match with what you want to manifest. You're no longer wanting from a place of separation; you're vibrating at the frequency of already having.

I start every session with my clients using this chart. We look at their current emotional states and compare them with their goals. This chart is more than just a way to see where they are; it's also a practical tool that clearly shows the gaps in their emotional energy. It highlights the differences between their current state and where they want to be and gives them a clear guide for starting the process of alignment. By illustrating these gaps, the chart provides a structured way for clients to start closing them, bringing them step-by-step in line with their desires.

This approach is powerful because it moves beyond just thinking about what you want and gets you to focus on how you'll feel when you have what you want. By tuning in to these feelings now, you're aligning yourself with the vibration of your desire. You're not just hoping or wishing anymore; you're actively creating the emotional foundation for your manifestation.

Remember, this isn't about denying your current feelings or pretending to be happy when you're not. It's about acknowledging where you are, understanding where you want to be, and then gradually shifting your emotional state. It's a process, and it takes practice. But with time and consistency, you'll find yourself naturally gravitating toward higher-vibrational states, making manifestation a more natural and effortless process.

Use this chart regularly. Check in with yourself daily. Where are you on the scale today? What can you do to move up, even just a little bit? Small shifts add up over time. As you practice, you'll become more aware of your emotional states and more skilled at consciously elevating them. This is the real work of manifestation—not just visualizing what you want, but becoming the person who already has it.

Heather's Story

When Heather first came to work with me, she was stuck in the London rat race, living in a one-bedroom apartment and grinding away at a demanding corporate job. With the city's sky-high property prices, she couldn't fathom how she'd ever afford a house with a yard. Her dream of freedom, greenery, and space to write felt impossibly out of reach. It was written all over her face. Here was someone desperately seeking freedom but feeling trapped in a life she couldn't escape.

In our first coaching session, she told me exactly what she wanted: "I want freedom. I want to be free of the shackles of a nine-to-five job. I want an author's life. In my vision, I have a desk looking out to a garden where I can see the clouds pass by and watch the wildlife in the trees. That's what I want. I don't want to be stuck in my one-bed apartment with a desk in the living room, looking out over a bus stop where pedestrians leave their discarded coffee cups and beer bottles on my wall. I want the freedom to wake up in the countryside and have no agenda other than to write."

We used the emotional vibrational chart during Heather's session to identify her emotions and where she wanted to be. Heather was feeling stuck, frustrated, and trapped. As we went through the exercise, it became clear that Heather's primary emotion associated with her dream life was freedom. This was our target: to raise her consciousness to align with the vibration of freedom. Her dream was clear, but it felt miles away from her reality. So we started an eight-week journey to help her understand the mechanics of manifestation.

Toward the end of our first session, I said something that caught her off guard: "This freedom that you crave, Heather, you could have some of it today."

"Really? But how?" she asked, trying to figure out what I was getting at.

I asked her, "Would you love an hour free every day to do as you wish?"

"Well, of course I would. But how?"

My advice was simple: "Take a lunch break. It's that simple. You desperately want this freedom; if you want it, you need to make space for it. Take a lunch break."

This might seem obvious to most people, but Heather had never allowed herself to take a break during her workday. She was chained to her desk, powering through without pause. The idea of stepping away for an hour was foreign to her. Heather later told me this piece of advice was a revelation. She even joked, "More annoyingly, why hadn't I thought of it myself? I've paid good money to be coached by someone who has told me to take a lunch hour—what the heck!" But sometimes, the simplest advice is the most powerful. That day, Heather left her apartment during work hours and walked to Greenwich Park. She bought a cappuccino, spent an hour with her thoughts, and returned to her desk feeling alive and creative. She'd gotten a taste of the freedom she craved.

As Heather consistently found ways to feel more freedom in her life, things started to shift. She began rehearsing her dream house and lifestyle during morning meditation, practicing gratitude, and journaling. As she did this, her energy and outlook started to shift. She wasn't just dreaming of freedom anymore but actively creating it daily. And that's when things got interesting.

In week three of our coaching, something incredible happened. Heather manifested her dream house. This wasn't just any house—it was exactly what she had been mentally rehearsing. The garden she'd visualized, the space for her writing desk, the freedom she'd been cultivating—it was all there. And get this: it was right across the street from where a friend of hers already lived. Heather had been looking for years without knowing how to buy a house in or near London. But because of our work, Heather found that feeling of freedom first and all the magic clicked together. Her friend called out of the blue to say a house nearby had just become available. It was on the outskirts of London in the countryside, with a short train ride into the city. It was exactly within Heather's budget, which she never thought possible. The previous owner, an artist, had passed away, and the family wanted to sell to someone who would love the place like their mom had. When Heather visited, she was stunned to see an owl statue in the garden. Heather loves owls. The seller, noticing her reaction, went upstairs and returned with a painting of two snowy owls that his mother had created. It was like the Universe was winking at Heather, confirming that this was indeed meant for her.

Even with these incredible synchronicities, fear still crept in. Heather had only ever known London life. Her body, programmed for the familiar, resisted the unknown. But the owl statue and the proximity to her friend were the signs she needed to lean in to that uncertainty.

This is what I mean by aligned, inspired action and cocreating with the Universe. Heather had been consistently feeling the freedom she desired, taking those lunch breaks, and visualizing her ideal space. When the opportunity presented itself, she was ready to act, even in fear. It wasn't about pretending she already had a house in the countryside. It was about cultivating the feeling of freedom that such a house represented. When Heather aligned her energy with that feeling, the Universe responded in the most magical way.

Heather's journey from being a stressed-out Londoner to manifesting her dream home highlights the importance of feeling your way to manifestation. It's not about faking it till you make it; it's about *feeling* it till you make it. Heather couldn't fake having the house, but she could nurture the feeling of freedom it represented before it appeared. That's what attracted experiences that matched that feeling.

This brings us to two important questions: If your feelings play such an important role in manifestation, how can you consciously create more feelings that are in alignment with your future desires? And how can you cultivate these feelings and integrate them within your normal day-to-day lifestyle?

PRACTICE:

Embody the Emotions Now

Now that you understand how crucial emotions and feelings are in manifestation, let's put this knowledge into action. Remember, cultivating specific emotions actively shapes your feelings, aligning your internal state with the reality you wish to create. Your goal is to consciously raise your emotional vibration until you're experiencing the feelings that would be present when your manifestation becomes a reality.

For instance, actively creating more gratitude increases your feelings of thankfulness and amplifies your overall sense of abundance and well-being. Similarly, nurturing emotions of love doesn't just fill you with affection but also enhances your connection to others and the world around you, making you feel more engaged and supported.

As you practice, you'll naturally start closing the gap between wanting and being, freeing yourself from the cycle of lack. Think about it: If you start feeling deeply connected to life, overflowing with gratitude or profoundly at peace, you'll no longer be waiting for external circumstances to bring those feelings into existence. Instead, you are creating them in your life right now.

To give you a clearer picture of our aim, I asked my followers to identify the key emotions they would feel when their desires manifested. Here, in no particular order, are the top ten most common high-vibrational emotions they shared:

- Freedom
- Happiness
- Joy
- Relief
- Peace
- Love
- Excitement
- Security
- Safety
- Gratitude

Step 1: Identify Your Emotions
First, identify three or four key emotions (or more if they naturally arise) that you believe you'll feel when your desire manifests. This might seem obvious, but trust me, it's worth taking the time to really think about it. Here's a little trick I use: I sit down for a focused meditation session during which I visualize

my future. As I do this, I pay close attention to how my body responds. What am I feeling? Where am I feeling it? After the session, I jot down any emotions, feelings, or physical sensations that popped up. These are your emotional signposts, guiding you toward the energy alignment you're aiming for.

Step 2: Cultivate These Emotions

Now, let's get creative. For each emotion you've chosen, brainstorm activities to help you feel that way in your daily life. Here are some ideas to get you started:

Freedom:
- Take a nonnegotiable break from work each day. Go for a walk or enjoy a meal. Just be sure you mentally disconnect from work.
- Spend twenty minutes daily without any digital distractions. Just sit, think, meditate, or breathe.
- Once a week, do something new. It could be as simple as trying a different coffee shop.

Gratitude:
- Kick off each day by listing five things you're grateful for.
- Set random alarms on your phone throughout the day, asking, "What am I grateful for right now?"
- Make it a habit to verbally express gratitude in everyday interactions.

Peace:
- Spend time in nature each week. It could be at a park, on the beach, or in your backyard.

- Create a calming bedtime routine. Read, listen to soft music, or do whatever helps you unwind.
- Schedule regular self-care activities. This could be getting a facial, enjoying a massage, or booking a spa day. Don't see it as a luxury; see it as investing in the energy that's part of your manifestation.

Excitement:
- Schedule regular date nights with your spouse or catchups with friends each week. Add it to your calendar; for example: Thursday between seven and ten p.m. is date night.
- Dust off an old hobby you used to love. Make time for it, and bring back the excitement, no matter how busy you are.
- Set up something small to look forward to each week, such as trying a new restaurant, watching a new movie, or taking the kids camping.

Abundance:
- Perform a random act of kindness daily, such as buying a stranger coffee or giving a genuine compliment.
- Whenever possible, help or mentor others. Sharing your knowledge and time can make you feel more abundant.
- Invest in your personal development with courses, books, or workshops.

Step 3: Implement and Track
Choose one activity for each emotion, and commit to it. Add these to your accountability practice. Consistency is key. At

first, it might feel like hard work and you might think, "This is ridiculous; I'm forcing myself to feel something." But stick with it. Before you know it, these practices will feel as natural as breathing. That's your brain rewiring itself, getting in sync with these higher vibes.

If you commit, you'll start to notice a shift. Those emotions you've been cultivating will start popping up on their own. It's like you're becoming emotionally aligned with your future self, the one who's already living your dream life.

And that's when the magic kicks in. You'll stumble upon synchronicities and spot opportunities that line up perfectly with your goals. You'll catch yourself taking inspired actions without even thinking about it. And here's the kicker: you'll start feeling like you already have what you're manifesting, even if it hasn't shown up in the physical world yet.

Step 4: Practice Emotional Awareness

Stay conscious of emotions that aren't in line with your manifestation. When you notice them, don't beat yourself up. Just gently guide yourself back to your chosen high-vibe emotions.

This can be tricky, especially if you're surrounded by people on different journeys. Your family or partner might inadvertently bring down your energy. The key is to stay aware of your own emotional frequency and not let others lower it. If you find yourself affected by others' lower vibes, that's okay. Become present and aware, and consciously choose to elevate your state again.

Here are some tricks I use:

1. **Set reminders on your phone to check in with your emotions throughout the day:** Schedule two or three random alerts with messages like "How am I feeling right now?" or "Align with gratitude for thirty seconds." These brief interruptions can help you reset your emotional state throughout the day.

2. **Create a visual cue in your environment that reminds you to realign when you see it:** This could be a piece of jewelry you wear daily, like a bracelet or a ring. Every time you notice it, use it as a trigger to check in with your emotions. Or keep a small photo of something that represents your desire in your wallet or on your desk. Whenever you see it, take a moment to align with the emotions of your desired outcome.

3. **Practice the STOP technique:**
   S—Stop
   T—Take a breath
   O—Observe your emotions
   P—Proceed mindfully

Remember, you're in charge of your own energy. You can't control others, but you can control how you respond to them.

Step 5: Release Trapped Emotion
Start by locating the feeling in your body. What does it feel like? Can you pinpoint where it is? Once you've found it, step back and become conscious of it. If you give it space, you'll allow it to escape. This is a gem I picked up from Dr. David

Hawkins's book *Letting Go.* We can only think equal to how we feel, so a suppressed feeling of fear will naturally lead to fearful thoughts, keeping us stuck.

There are loads of tools to help you release trapped energy and level up your emotional state. We've talked about meditation, and I'll dive into journaling in the next chapter. Another technique I swear by is the Emotional Freedom Technique (EFT). This method involves gently tapping specific meridian points on your body while consciously focusing on thoughts or emotions. It's based on the same energy meridians used in traditional acupuncture to treat physical and emotional ailments but without the invasiveness of needles.

When I feel triggered or when my energy feels heavy, I use tapping to help release the emotions and elevate my vibration. By doing so, EFT tapping not only reduces stress and manages anxiety, but also clears mental clutter, allowing for clearer thinking and better decision-making. Moreover, EFT tapping can be particularly effective in restoring your mind to a flow state. In this state, you're more open to receiving creative ideas and inspired actions, which are key components of successful manifestation. If you are interested in incorporating this technique into your manifestation routine, you can find tons of resources on YouTube to learn more.

CHAPTER 8

Journaling

P utting pen to paper is more than just a writing exercise; it's a transformative act that turns thoughts into reality. This is the essence of journaling for manifestation. It's not about recording events; it's about confronting fears, challenging yourself, reflecting deeply, dreaming, planning strategically, and taking inspired action.

For five years, I've made journaling a nonnegotiable part of my daily routine, as essential as brushing my teeth. I write daily, without exception—on Christmas, birthdays, and days with early flights. This unwavering habit has given me unprecedented control over my energy and the direction of my life.

Think about those times you've felt stuck or frustrated. Those feelings don't simply evaporate; they simmer beneath the surface, quietly sabotaging your manifestation efforts. Journaling acts as your emotional release valve. It's the safe space where you can voice the thoughts you've been afraid to acknowledge, even to yourself.

True manifestation requires more than just positive thinking. It demands healing from past wounds and clearing stagnant energy. Many of us unknowingly hold on to energy that manifests as frustration, anxiety, or even physical ailments. When we bottle up our emotions, we're not just suppressing feelings, we're trapping energy that needs to flow. This stagnant energy can act as a blockade to our manifestations, keeping us stuck in patterns we're trying to break free from. Journaling provides the outlet we desperately need.

This practice is as transformative as it is therapeutic. It rewires your brain and realigns your energy with your desires. Each time you put pen to paper, you heal a little more. When you heal, you release. When you release, you raise your energy to match that of your future self—the one who's already living your dream life.

In a world that constantly tries to distract you and mold you into someone you're not, your journal is the one place where you get to be unapologetically you. It's your war room for battling self-doubt, your laboratory for experimenting with new ideas, and your sanctuary for planning your dreams.

When facing challenges or complex manifestations, I turn to my journal, asking probing questions: What's holding me back? What's blocking me? Why do I feel this way? What action can I take? I typically dedicate about twenty minutes each morning to this practice. Some days it's shorter and on others it's longer, but

I never miss a day. My routine has remained consistent for years—sitting upright in bed, free from distractions, with Corisande journaling beside me. There's a palpable energy in the room as we write, sometimes in contemplative silence and at other times with our future playlists playing softly through headphones.

Authenticity is the cornerstone of effective journaling. Be ruthlessly honest with yourself as you write. Become a detached observer of your own thoughts and feelings, asking ever deeper questions: Why am I struggling with this particular issue? What's the root cause of my inability to move forward? This self-inquiry helps uncover and heal deep-seated blocks, clearing the path for powerful manifestation.

Digital methods can be effective, yet there's a unique power in handwriting for manifestation. Think back to the last hand-written letter you received; the sender's energy seems to linger on the paper in a way no email or text can replicate. That's why pen-to-paper journaling is so crucial in manifestation work. It's like sending a handwritten letter to the Universe, carrying your intentions or releasing trapped emotions with every stroke of the pen.

I approach journaling in three distinct ways, which are each uniquely powerful:

1. Stream of consciousness
2. Scripting
3. Prompts

Stream of Consciousness

The first approach to journaling is what I refer to as stream of consciousness. Julia Cameron popularized this technique in her book *The Artist's Way*, calling it "morning pages." It's exactly what it sounds like—a free-flowing, unfiltered outpouring of your thoughts onto paper. As you sit down, pen in hand, you allow anything to come up. Words flow, sometimes surprising you, comforting you, or upsetting you. It's raw. You just go with the flow as your pen moves across the page. You might find yourself smiling at a happy memory or feeling a sense of relief as you finally articulate a fear that's been lurking in the back of your mind.

There's no specific prompt, action plan, structure, or goal other than to write. It's just you and the page. That fear holding you back? Write it down. The nagging thoughts about your never-ending to-do list? Write them down. A sudden childhood memory? That weird dream you had last night? It goes on the page. You're not trying to solve anything or reach conclusions. You're simply emptying your mind onto the page, like turning on a tap and letting the water run clear.

I've found this approach to be a lifeline, especially when I'm feeling off but can't quite put my finger on why. In those moments, I write. I don't know what will happen, but I trust the process. It's incredible how often I find clarity or unexpected solutions by letting my thoughts flow.

This is more than writing and clearing your mind; it's about healing, resetting, and finding balance. Manifestation isn't always about pushing forward and taking action; sometimes it's about stopping, slowing down, and clearing the path. Stream-of-consciousness writing does this beautifully, helping you stay in harmony with life, process emotions, release pent-up energy, and make space for new possibilities.

This is where you let out those little annoyances, worries, and frustrations that build up over time. If you're ever feeling off or like you've woken up on the wrong side of the bed and can't understand why, write. You'll find that the answers, which might be lying dormant beyond your conscious awareness, tend to emerge. When you do this, it becomes a form of meditation. It's therapeutic to quiet mental chatter by giving it somewhere to go.

Don't worry about grammar, spelling, or even making sense. The goal isn't to create a masterpiece—it's to create a space for your unfiltered self to exist. These pages are for your eyes only. It's about giving yourself the freedom to be authentically you on the page. My advice is to not overthink it. Trust the process and allow your intuition to guide your hand. You might uncover insights you didn't know you had or make connections between seemingly unrelated thoughts.

For many, journaling has become more than a technique; it's a lifeline in their manifestation journey. I was reminded of this recently during dinner with Corisande. We were reflecting on our manifestation journey and all the different tools we've discovered along the way. As we shared stories over our meal, we found ourselves laughing about her ongoing battle with patience—it had become her signature challenge in manifestation. "Patience has always been my weakest point," she admitted, smiling. "Manifestation can be challenging because it feels like putting my desires into the open air and then waiting in uncertainty. The hardest part is that period between setting an intention and seeing it manifest."

Unlike letting go, journaling provides something tangible and concrete for her. "Each day, as I put pen to paper, I'm reaffirming my intentions, reinforcing my faith, and soothing my impatience. It makes my intentions feel present and alive, even if they haven't yet materialized." During difficult times, journaling provides a safe space to express emotions she might not be ready to voice aloud. In moments of happiness, it captures memories to revisit with inspiration and pride. "Looking back, I see my journey of growth and resilience documented in my own handwriting. The moment the ink meets the paper, my thoughts become real and lasting. Once I close the journal and put down my pen, I feel a sense of release and trust. I don't dwell on what I've written; I let it go, knowing the Universe has heard me."

Through journaling, she's completely transformed her relationship with patience. Now, whenever she feels that familiar impatience creeping in, she turns straight to her journal and writes it all out. What was once her biggest trigger has become a pathway to deeper self-awareness and trust in the manifestation process.

As you practice stream-of-consciousness writing, you might find yourself naturally shifting toward more focused, intentional writing. Sometimes, your free-flowing thoughts start to paint a picture of your ideal future. This is where you begin to bridge the gap between unstructured journaling and a more deliberate manifestation technique known as *scripting*.

Scripting

Scripting is precisely what it sounds like—you're writing the script of your ideal life as if it's already happening. It's not just daydreaming; it's a deliberate act of conscious creation that allows you to step into the shoes of your future self and experience your desired reality in vivid detail. The key is to write in the present tense as if everything you want has already come to fruition.

In chapter 6, we discussed scripting as a form of mental rehearsal. Now, let's delve deeper into this technique and explore how I've optimized its use in my own practice. Here's my approach: I imagine the scene where my future self has achieved everything I'm trying to manifest. Then, I hand over the pen to that version of me. It usually begins something like this: "Life is incredible. Everything has fallen into place beautifully, just as I knew it would. The unknown didn't let me down; the Universe had my back, and all the pieces fell into place in divine time. All I needed to do was surrender and trust the process."

From there, I let the pen take over and start writing about a specific part of my future self's life. It might be a scene from my perfect day or what it felt like receiving news about something I'm currently working on manifesting. That's the beauty of scripting: it's a timeline in the future where everything has worked out. I love to describe where I'm living, what's around me, what I'm doing, my surroundings, my feelings, my accomplishments, the people in my life, the work I'm doing, and the impact I'm making. The more detail, the better.

To ramp up the experience, I play my future playlist while writing. Putting on headphones and losing yourself on the page becomes a second form of meditation. This combination of music and writing creates an immersive experience that can truly transform your manifestation practice. For me, it's a super-charged meditation—the feelings are cultivated more quickly than usual.

Remember, scripting isn't about perfection; it's about feeling. So let the emotions flow as you write. Allow yourself to experience the joy, gratitude, and sense of accomplishment of living your ideal life. These emotions are the fuel that powers your manifestations. If you're struggling to "believe" while doing this, don't worry. It's a common challenge. The key is to start where you are. You don't have to script your ultimate dream life right away. Instead, consider scripting as your future self who's just one step ahead.

For example, if you're about to hand in your resignation and feeling nervous, your script might start like this: "I did it. I handed in my resignation letter today. My hands were shaking a bit, but I felt this incredible sense of relief and excitement as soon as I did it. My boss was understanding, and now I feel like I'm finally on the path to pursuing my true passion."

Or perhaps you're building up the courage to ask someone out on a date: "I can't believe I actually did it. I asked George out for coffee, and he said yes! My heart was pounding, but when the words left my mouth, I felt so proud of myself for taking that leap."

By breaking down your bigger manifestations into smaller,

more believable steps, you're making the process more manageable and accessible for you to truly feel and believe.

Scripting was incredibly powerful when any manifestation felt hard or tested my patience. There's something magical about doing this first thing in the morning before the day's distractions creep in. It sets the tone for your entire day, aligning your energy with your desires from the moment you wake up.

Remember, the goal is to cultivate a sense of expectation that your writing has come true while also practicing the art of letting go. Stay open to the outcomes and how they will come about. Trust that as you align your energy through this practice, the Universe will conspire to bring your desires to life, often in ways more amazing than you could have scripted yourself.

Now, as powerful as scripting is, there are days when you need more structure or guidance in your journaling practice. That's where prompts come in. They serve as a bridge between the free-flowing nature of stream-of-consciousness writing and the future-focused approach of scripting.

Prompts

Prompts are questions or statements that spark deep reflection. They're targeted tools to help you explore your inner world, face your fears, and uncover what you might be hiding from yourself. The power of prompts is in their ability to direct your energy. Where attention goes, energy flows. Prompts give me a laser-focused way to channel that energy. It's just me and the question—

no fluff, no distractions. I'm drilling down into specific aspects of my life and journey.

I alternate between self-observational and future-oriented prompts, which creates a balance in my practice. Self-observational prompts clarify your current state, while future-oriented prompts align with your desired reality. They're like conversing with yourself, diving deep into your thoughts, feelings, and aspirations. When you're stuck or need to dig deeper, these prompts are your lifeline.

Imagine sitting down with a prompt like, "What's the most difficult conversation I need to have with myself?" Suddenly, you're engaged. Focused. You're exploring every angle of that question. It's a powerful way to bridge the gap between where you are and where you want to be.

I switch up my prompts daily, with just one question each day. This keeps me balanced, one foot in the present and one in the future. It's like staying on the baseline in tennis, ready for anything. Self-observational prompts ground you. They help you spot patterns, identify blocks, and recognize signs guiding you.

On the other hand, future-oriented prompts keep you aligned with your vision. They connect you to your desires, challenge you to act, and encourage you to confront the fears and aspects that hold you back. They help refine your vision and ask more significant questions, ensuring you're always moving toward your dreams.

This approach is disciplined yet flexible. Some days you need more grounding, and on other days you need more inspiration. You adapt and find the prompts that best suit your journey.

Here are ten self-observational prompts I regularly use:

- What thought patterns have I noticed in myself recently?

- What's the wisest voice in my head been saying that I've been ignoring?

- What's one small win I have had recently that I haven't given myself credit for?

- What part of myself must I love and accept to move forward?

- What's the most challenging truth I must tell someone to move forward?

- In what ways am I still living someone else's life rather than my own?

- What's the most difficult conversation I need to have with myself?

- What outdated version of myself am I still loyal to? How can I let it go?

- If I let go of all of my fear, what would I do that I don't do now?

- What patterns in my life do I keep repeating? What lesson am I refusing to learn?

While self-observational prompts ground us in the present, future-oriented prompts propel us forward, aligning us with our highest potential. These questions invite us to step into the shoes of our future selves, to see through their eyes and feel with their hearts. They bridge the gap between who we are and what we want, deliberately helping us move beyond wanting.

Here are ten future-self alignment prompts I regularly use:

- How would I approach my biggest challenge if I knew I couldn't fail?

- My future self can erase one habit I currently have. Which one will they choose to delete and why?

- What new chapter do I want to start in my life? Describe it in detail, imagining it as vividly as possible.

- What boundaries has my future self set to protect their time and energy?

- How can I take inspired action this week in alignment with my vision?

- What would I do differently this week if I knew I couldn't fail?

- How would my future self think, act, feel, and show up today?

- Describe a goal I think is out of reach. Now, break it down: What are the first three actions I can take to make it a reality?

- What am I avoiding out of fear, and how can I face it and step outside my comfort zone?

- How can I raise my vibration today?

These prompts are my go-to favorites that have helped me on my journey. You should start with these to kick-start your own practice. As you progress, you'll naturally develop prompts that best serve your unique path. You'll find other prompts on my social media accounts to help provoke deep thought and reflection. However, finding prompts that align with your specific intentions is critical. Whether health-related, financial, fitness-focused, or centered on love and relationships, remember that everyone's manifestation journey is unique. The goal is to find your own stride and discover what works best for you.

As you explore these prompts and develop your own, you'll notice patterns, insights, and shifts in your thinking. This is the power of consistent journaling. It's not just about writing; it's about uncovering truths and shaping your reality.

PRACTICE:

Daily Manifestation Journal

Now that we've explored the power of journaling and three techniques, it's time to implement this knowledge. I challenge you to incorporate journaling into your daily routine and hold yourself accountable.

Here's how to get started:

Step 1: Choose Your Tools

Invest in a journal and pen that excite you. I know this sounds simple, but trust me, it makes all the difference. The feel of quality paper and a pen that glides smoothly can transform your writing experience from a chore to a cherished ritual.

Step 2: Set a Daily Appointment with Yourself

Whether it's after meditation, during your lunch break, or before bed, choose a consistent time. Make this nonnegotiable, like brushing your teeth. Find a time and location, and commit to it.

Step 3: Rotate Your Approach

Alternate stream of consciousness, scripting, and prompts as you write. This variety keeps your practice fresh and allows you to explore different aspects of yourself and your goals.

Step 4: Commit to Sixty-Six Days

As discussed in chapter 5, sixty-six days is the sweet spot for forming a new habit. Make this your initial goal, and add it to your daily accountability. By day sixty-seven, you might find that you can't imagine starting your day without your journal.

Step 5: Be Ruthlessly Honest

Your journal is your safe space. No one else will read it. Use this privacy to be completely truthful with yourself. Let your deepest fears, wildest dreams, and rawest emotions flow onto the page.

Remember, trust your intuition. Follow that instinct if a particular prompt or method calls to you on a given day. Your inner wisdom knows what you need.

As we close this chapter, I want you to ask yourself: "Can I afford not to journal? Can I risk leaving my dreams to chance?" This is your life we're talking about. It's time to pick up that pen and start writing.

CHAPTER 9

Gratitude

An experience with gratitude completely transformed my understanding of manifestation during a pivotal moment in our lives. Corisande and I had just finished renovating a two-hundred-year-old cottage and were ready to put it on the market. While we were proud of our work, a cloud of doubt hung over us as we prepared to sell. It wasn't your run-of-the-mill property. Far from it. We'd bought it four years earlier after it had been collecting cobwebs on the market for more than five years. Picture this: a quirky mid-terrace cottage awkwardly sandwiched between two other houses, looking like it couldn't decide which one it belonged to. From the street, it was a real head-scratcher, the kind of place you either fall head over heels for or run away from screaming. We had done a great job of making the inside look good, but we couldn't help but be aware of all of its exterior pitfalls. To complicate matters further, it had a possessory title, meaning the previous owner had lost the title deed, which added another layer of complication to the sale.

Every negative thought raced through my mind as we prepared to put it on the market. Who would want to buy such an unconventional property? Should we just rent it out instead? Would we ever see the equity we'd invested? It was at this moment of doubt that a book fell into my lap that would change everything: *The Magic* by Rhonda Byrne. In it, Byrne wrote beautifully about how gratitude has been practiced across different civilizations and religions for thousands of years, and this opened my eyes to a whole new way of practicing gratitude. But what caught my attention was her suggestion to use gratitude for something you're seeking to manifest before it manifests. I had practiced gratitude before, but it had always been rather basic. My gratitude lists typically looked something like this:

- I am grateful for my wife.
- I am grateful for the roof over my head.
- I am grateful for my health.

If I'm being honest, I hadn't fully grasped the power behind gratitude for manifestation. I understood that elevating our emotional state to gratitude was powerful, but I had yet to see much tangible proof of material desires manifesting until Byrne suggested using gratitude for things yet to manifest or for solutions to problems.

It was as if a light had suddenly illuminated a path I hadn't seen before. I immediately understood the paradox: we must embody the end result now in order for it to manifest. Waiting for my manifestations to appear before expressing thankfulness kept me in a state of lack and separation. I needed to start expressing gratitude as if my desires had already manifested to transcend this wanting paradox.

I decided to apply this new understanding of gratitude to the sale of our house. Instead of being grateful for what we already had, I expressed gratitude for each step of the selling process before it happened. I started by reverse engineering the entire house sale process into small, individual steps. I did this because I had doubt about selling the property, so each step would align with the overall main intention of selling the house, regardless of how small the step.

It began with being thankful that the agent would value the property above our expectations. Then, I expressed gratitude for selling the property within the first weekend it was on the market to a cash buyer.

To my astonishment, these exact scenarios unfolded. The property was valued higher than we expected. Within the first weekend of viewings, we received an offer from a retired cash buyer in her late sixties, precisely as I had envisioned in my gratitude practice. But I didn't stop there. I continued to use gratitude throughout the entire selling process, expressing thanks for a sympathetic surveyor, a smooth legal process, and a quick completion. Each step of the way, reality aligned with what I had expressed gratitude for in advance.

I was astounded. Like magic, gratitude worked in every aspect of the process.

This experience ignited a deep curiosity about how gratitude was the most effective of all the manifestation tools. Since that moment, I began to use gratitude in this way for all aspects of my life, what I call "closing the gap" or "collapsing the wave" between where I am and where I want to be. It's been an invaluable tool and instrumental in manifesting my dream life. In fact, although mental rehearsal played a vital role, gratitude was foundational for manifesting this book you are reading.

Gratitude is more than just an emotion; it's a state of being that acknowledges receipt. Looking at the emotional vibrational chart in chapter 7, you'll see that gratitude sits high up there, alongside emotions like love and freedom. But gratitude is unique in its power to manifest.

Think about it. When do we usually express gratitude in our daily lives? It's when we receive something positive. When someone gives us a gift, our immediate response is "Thank you." When we get good news, we might exclaim, "Yes! That's brilliant news!" followed by a "Thank you." In these moments, we're in a state of receivership, acknowledging and appreciating what has come into our lives.

This is precisely why gratitude is such a powerful tool for manifestation. As we've discussed, the Universe aligns with what you are, not what you want. It responds to your vibration, your emotional state, and your being. When you express gratitude for something you desire as if you've already received it, you put yourself in that state of receivership before the physical manifestation has occurred.

This is exactly what happened with the sale of our cottage. By expressing gratitude for each step of the process before it happened, I aligned myself with the reality where these events had already occurred. I told the Universe, "This is already in my life, and I'm profoundly thankful for it." And the Universe, in turn, began to align circumstances to match this vibration.

In my journey from selling that quirky cottage to manifesting this book and beyond, I've seen time and again how this approach can dramatically accelerate the manifestation process. Combining this profound emotional alignment with practical steps creates a powerful synergy that brings our desires into reality.

Structuring Gratitude Statements

Through practice and refinement, I've developed a method for structuring gratitude statements that works best for me. I no longer use simple bullet points. Instead, I have a framework, influenced by Byrne's teachings, and I consistently use five gratitude statements daily. The way gratitude statements are structured is crucial to their effectiveness. Here's the formula I use:

1. Start with "I am so grateful now that . . ."
2. Include "because . . ."
3. Explain why you are grateful.
4. Finish with "Thank you, thank you, thank you."

This structure is designed to engage both your conscious and subconscious mind, creating a powerful emotional resonance that amplifies your manifestation intentions.

Let's look at a few examples for everyday life:

"I am so grateful now that I've been invited for an interview at [company name] because this opportunity brings me one step closer to creating the life I envision for my family. Thank you, thank you, thank you."

"I am so grateful now that I've found the perfect mentor because their wisdom and experience will accelerate my growth, helping me overcome obstacles and achieve my goals more efficiently. Thank you, thank you, thank you."

"I am so grateful now that unexpected money has started flowing into my life because it allows me to enjoy life's pleasures and invest in my future dreams. Thank you, thank you, thank you."

Now, let's break down each component of these statements:

- Part 1: "I am so grateful now that . . .": This is the intention. In manifestation, this sparks the vision, engaging the conscious mind—the creative part of the brain that generates ideas and knows what it wants. When you write this phrase, you activate this part of your brain, setting the stage for manifestation.
- Part 2: "because": This powerful word acts as a bridge between your conscious and subconscious mind. It takes your intention and connects it to your body, to the feeling.
- Part 3: The "why": This is where you explain the reason for your gratitude. It's the emotional core of

your statement, tying your intention to a deeper purpose or feeling.

- Part 4: "Thank you, thank you, thank you": This triple expression of gratitude, which I picked up from Byrne, is a bit of fun, but I've integrated it into my practice. It amplifies the feeling of gratitude and acts as a powerful closing to your statement.

In my practice, I vary my gratitude statements between simple pleasures we often take for granted—my family, health, and present blessings—and things I'm actively working to manifest.

Typically, out of my five daily gratitude statements, at least two or three are dedicated to things I'm actively manifesting. This approach helps me stay balanced, maintaining momentum in my manifestation practice while cultivating a deep appreciation for my current blessings.

The Power of *Because*

Psychologist Ellen Langer and her colleagues at Harvard conducted a fascinating study that revealed the profound influence of the word *because* on human behavior. They were interested in exploring how people make quick decisions in everyday situations and what verbal cues might influence these choices. The experiment, elegantly simple yet profoundly insightful, took place at a university library where people often lined up to use copy machines. The researchers crafted a clever set of requests to see how the word *because* might affect people's willingness to let someone cut in line.

They enlisted the help of students who approached people in the line for the copy machine with one of three requests:

1. "Excuse me, I have five pages. May I use the copy machine?"
2. "Excuse me, I have five pages. May I use the copy machine because I'm in a rush?"
3. "Excuse me, I have five pages. May I use the copy machine because I have to make copies?"

The results, gathered over one hundred twenty trials, were astounding: When no reason was given (request 1), only 60 percent of people let the person cut in line. With a genuine reason (request 2), a whopping 94 percent of people stepped aside. Surprisingly, even with a reason that simply repeated the obvious (request 3), 93 percent of people still allowed line-jumping!

Intrigued by these findings, Langer and her team decided to push the boundaries further. They increased the request from five pages to twenty pages. The results shifted dramatically: With no reason, only 24 percent let them cut in line. With a genuine reason ("because I'm in a rush"), 42 percent allowed them to go ahead. With the obvious reason ("because I have to make copies"), only 24 percent stepped aside. This shift highlights a crucial aspect of human psychology: the magic of *because* works best when asking for something small and easy to agree to. When the stakes are higher, our analytical minds kick in and we're less likely to be swayed by a flimsy reason.

But why does this because effect happen? The researchers think it's all about how our brains evolved to make quick decisions. The first evolutionary phenomenon is shortcut thinking—our brains love these mental shortcuts. When we hear *because*, it's like a trigger that says, "Hey, an explanation is coming!" Our brain often accepts this explanation without much questioning, especially for small requests. This connects to our survival instinct. Think about our ancestors—understanding why things happened was crucial for survival. "Because there's a predator" was much more useful than just "Run!" Our need to understand why is deeply ingrained. Explanations serve as social glue, helping us get along with others. When someone gives us a reason, even a flimsy one, we're more likely to cooperate. It's like a social lubricant that makes interactions smoother. In essence, *because* taps into our brain's desire for efficiency and our deep-seated need to understand the world around us. It's like a magic word that often gets our subconscious to nod along, even before our conscious mind has a chance to think it through.

As a result, we've developed a mental shortcut: when we hear *because*, we tend to accept what comes next without thinking too deeply about it. This automatic acceptance is our brain's way of saving energy. It helps us cope with everyday situations quickly, without having to think too hard about each little decision.

Langer and her team realized that we often respond more to how things are said than what's actually being said, particularly when we're not putting in much mental effort. It's as if our brains have this built-in craving for explanations, even if those explanations are flimsy when you really think about them.

Now, here's where it gets exciting for manifestation and gratitude. When we craft our gratitude statements, we're essentially using the same powerful formula from Langer's experiment: "I am grateful for [intention] because [reason/emotion]." By including *because* in our gratitude practice, we're not just listing things we're thankful for; we're giving our subconscious mind a reason to believe in our gratitude.

This *because* is like a bridge connecting our conscious intention with the deeper, more emotional part of our minds. It's not just about being thankful; it's about aligning our gratitude with our core desires and motivations. By using *because* in our gratitude statements, we open a powerful channel to our subconscious mind, potentially bypassing the skeptical voice that says "But it hasn't happened yet."

This is where things get interesting. Remember the PEAR experiment from chapter 5? The PEAR researchers suggested that our subconscious mind has more influence over physical reality than our conscious, analytical mind. Now, imagine harnessing that power in your manifestation practice. By speaking directly to your subconscious through carefully structured gratitude statements, you could be tapping into a wellspring of manifestation potential that you never knew you had.

This is where I started to connect the dots. If the subconscious mind can influence physical reality more effectively when it's not hindered by analytical thinking, and if *because* helps bypass our analytical mind, could this be the key to understanding the magic of gratitude in manifestation? I think so.

Why Simplicity Wins with Gratitude

You've probably heard the advice to "Think big" and set goals that scare you. This approach works wonders for some, but I've noticed a common stumbling block. When my clients set these grand intentions, there's often a moment of hesitation, a split second during which disbelief flashes across their face before they commit it to paper. It's right there that most people trip up. If your goal feels unbelievable, it's hard to stay aligned and easier to stay stuck in wanting mode, which, as we now understand, is a lack.

Here's the thing: having a grand vision is important, but it's not a one-size-fits-all solution. For some people, an audacious goal ignites an unwavering belief that propels them forward. But for others, it can actually hinder the manifestation process. Why? Because when a goal feels too far out of reach, it becomes difficult to maintain emotional alignment with it.

Imagine standing at the base of Mount Everest, trying to envision yourself at the peak. The sheer magnitude of the task can be overwhelming. This is what happens when we focus solely on a massive goal—it often highlights the gap between where we are and where we want to be. This distance can feel insurmountable, making it challenging to genuinely believe in the outcome and stay emotionally connected to it. That's why I often challenge people to reverse engineer their main goals into smaller, more manageable aspects. It might seem counterintuitive, but this approach can accelerate the manifestation of your larger desire. Here's why:

1. It keeps you in better alignment: Smaller goals are easier to believe in and emotionally connect with.
2. It creates momentum: Achieving smaller goals builds confidence and reinforces your belief in the manifestation process.
3. It closes the gap: By focusing on the next step rather than the end goal, you're constantly moving beyond the wanting stage.

Think of it as climbing rungs on a ladder. Your big goal is at the top, but instead of fixating on that distant peak, you concentrate on ascending one rung at a time. This approach aligns perfectly with Langer's study, which showed that smaller requests were more effective in gaining compliance. In my experience with manifestation, breaking down goals into smaller steps and using *because* in gratitude statements for these steps yields remarkable results.

Here's how to approach this: Start with your big goal, such as landing your dream job at a specific company. Next, break it down into steps—updating your résumé, networking with industry professionals, securing an interview, preparing for it, receiving an offer, negotiating, accepting, and nailing your first month. Each of these becomes a smaller manifestation in its own right—more immediate, more believable, and easier to align with emotionally.

Now here's where the magic happens. Focus on the next rung of that ladder, expressing gratitude for it until it manifests. For instance: "I am so grateful now that I've updated my résumé because it perfectly showcases my skills and experience. Thank you, thank you, thank you." Once this manifests, move to the next step: "I am so grateful now that I've been invited to an industry networking event because it's an opportunity to make meaningful connections in my desired field. Thank you, thank you, thank you."

Treat this as a journey, always focusing on the next achievable step across various areas of your life. This gratitude statement for your current manifestation step will be just one of your five daily gratitude statements.

My theory is that when we use *because* in our gratitude statements and focus on the next sequential step, we create a direct line between our conscious desires and our subconscious mind. The *because* is a bridge, bypassing our analytical, often skeptical brain and sinking deeper into our subconscious. From there, these intentions communicate more directly with the Universe. It's as if the subconscious, free from doubt and analytical resistance, can broadcast our desires on a frequency the Universe readily receives and responds to.

This approach doesn't mean you can't dream big. It's about finding the right balance between your grand vision and the practical steps needed to get there. By breaking down your big goals and using targeted gratitude statements, you're setting yourself up for a manifestation journey that's both exciting and achievable.

It's crucial to remember that we're still leaving the actual manifestation of each step to the Universe. We're simply treating these steps as smaller aspects of the larger intention, like stepping stones. Each of these smaller manifestations is still part of manifesting the bigger goal. We're not controlling the how or when.

That's not our conscious job. Instead, we're setting smaller intentions and using gratitude to get into a state of "already having."

This is exactly how I manifest, and I've seen the results. Don't let anyone tell you differently. By focusing on these smaller aspects, we're not limiting our dreams; we're creating a clear path for them to unfold in ways that might surprise and delight us. The Universe still has plenty of room to work its magic, bringing opportunities and synchronicities we might never have imagined. Our job is to stay aligned, grateful, and open to receiving.

PRACTICE:

The Magic of Gratitude

Now that we've explored how gratitude can supercharge your manifestation efforts, let's put this knowledge into action. This daily ritual will help you harness the magic of gratitude to manifest your desires, one step at a time, keeping you aligned and in vibrational resonance with your goals.

Step 1: Prepare Your Manifestation Ladder

- List your main manifestation goals. These might include buying your dream home, meeting your soulmate, landing your dream job, or achieving specific business success.
- Place your ultimate goal at the top of your ladder.
- Break down this goal into five to ten smaller, sequential steps. Each step should feel more achievable than the big manifestation itself.

- Arrange these steps on the rungs below your ultimate goal, starting with the first step from where you are now.
- Write this out, creating your personal "manifestation ladder."

Step 2: Integrate Gratitude into Your Daily Routine

- Add this gratitude practice to your accountability routine. Consistency is key in forming new habits, so commit to this practice for at least sixty-six days.
- Choose a consistent time for your daily gratitude practice. I do mine at 6:30 a.m., right after meditation and journaling.

Step 3: Establish a Daily Gratitude Practice

- Every day, write five gratitude statements in your journal. You can structure these statements in whatever way feels most aligned with your journey. Some days you might focus entirely on current blessings, while other days might be more focused on future manifestations. Here's one suggested way to structure your practice:
- Write three statements focused on your current blessings or things you're genuinely thankful for.
- Write one statement for the next step on your manifestation ladder.
- Write one statement for another area of your life you're working on manifesting.
- Use this structure: "I am so grateful now that [intention] because [reason/emotion]. Thank you, thank you, thank you."

Step 4: Visualize and Feel
- After writing each statement, close your eyes and visualize what you're expressing gratitude for.
- Really feel the emotion of gratitude as if it has already happened.
- Try saying "Thank you" aloud and placing your hand over your heart to reinforce the feeling. This helps me.

Step 5: Take Aligned, Inspired Action
- Be open to opportunities related to your gratitude statements throughout your day.
- Act on these opportunities, no matter how small they seem.
- Stay present and aware of any signs or synchronicities related to your gratitude focus.

Step 6: Celebrate Each Rung on the Ladder
- When a step manifests, celebrate it. Journal about it, reflect, and treat yourself.
- Move to the next rung on your ladder, always aware of how it connects to your ultimate goal.

Final Thoughts on Gratitude

As you embark on this gratitude journey, it's worth considering a powerful parallel from the world of personal finance. Dave Ramsey, a renowned financial adviser, teaches a concept called the *debt snowball* to help people get out of debt. In this approach, people list their debts from smallest to largest, focusing on paying off the smallest debt first while maintaining minimum payments on the others. As they pay off each debt, they move to the next, creating momentum and a sense of accomplishment.

The debt snowball method aligns beautifully with our gratitude-driven manifestation approach. Just as Ramsey encourages people to focus on the smallest debt first, I encourage you to break down your ultimate manifestation goal into smaller, more manageable steps. Your big goal—whether it's being debt-free, buying your dream house, or achieving a major career milestone—sits at the top of your ladder. But your focus remains on the next achievable rung.

The beauty of this approach lies in its ability to create a sense of progress and accomplishment. When you focus solely on a big, distant goal, it's easy to feel overwhelmed or discouraged by your apparent lack of progress. But by breaking it down and celebrating each small victory along the way, you maintain momentum and stay motivated.

In the context of gratitude and manifestation, this means expressing thankfulness for each small step as it manifests. Each rung you climb is a victory worth celebrating. This consistent acknowledgment of progress keeps you in a positive, receptive state, making it easier to attract the next step on your journey.

Remember, manifestation is not about waiting or wanting. It's about aligning your energy with the reality you wish to create in the present moment. Gratitude is the key that unlocks this alignment. Each "Thank you" is a powerful affirmation that you're open and ready to receive the abundance the Universe has to offer. It's about feeling completely whole and grateful for your life's blessings while genuinely believing and feeling that the next step on your manifestation journey has already manifested. By doing this, your state is receptive, meaning that more energy aligned to that state will collapse into your physical reality.

This is the true beauty of gratitude-driven manifestation—it keeps you in constant forward motion, always progressing. Some steps may manifest with breathtaking speed, while others might unfold more gradually. Yet each one, regardless of its pace, plays a vital role in your journey.

CHAPTER 10

Affirmations

In the early 1900s, French pharmacist Émile Coué made a discovery that would revolutionize our understanding of the mind's power. Coué's journey began in his pharmacy in Troyes, France, where he observed a fascinating phenomenon: patients who believed they would get better often did, regardless of their medication. Intrigued by this mind-body connection, Coué started experimenting. He became known for reassuring his clients by praising each remedy's effectiveness and including a small positive note with each medication. Patients who received these encouraging messages seemed to respond better to treatment and heal faster. Driven by these results, Coué studied hypnosis in Nancy, France, in 1885 and 1886. He was searching for ways to harness the power of suggestion more effectively. Although hypnosis showed promise, Coué felt it had limitations, primarily because it required the presence of a hypnotist. He believed there must be a more universal way to use the power of the mind—one that patients could apply themselves.

After extensive research and experimentation, Coué developed his method of "conscious autosuggestion." This approach, similar to what we now call affirmations, involves repeating positive statements to influence the mind. He distilled it into a simple phrase: "Every day, in every way, I'm getting better and better." He instructed his patients to repeat this twenty times each night before bed and each morning after waking. Coué chose these times because the conscious mind is less active then, making it easier to reach what he called the "unconscious" mind, which we now refer to as the subconscious.

To help his patients keep count of their positive statements, Coué recommended using a string with twenty knots. As patients repeated the phrase, they would move their fingers along the string, one knot at a time. This simple tool helped them maintain focus and ensured the complete twenty repetitions. Coué emphasized that the phrase should be repeated mechanically, without force or will, allowing the suggestion to bypass the critical faculty of the conscious mind and plant itself directly in the subconscious.

The results of Coué's method were remarkable. Patients with various conditions began to show significant improvements. Those struggling with physical ailments reported relief, while others found new mental and emotional resilience. One particularly inspiring case was that of a twenty-two-year-old girl who had suffered from epileptic fits since childhood. Her seizures had been recurring at different intervals every couple of weeks, disrupting her life. After her first visit to Coué's clinic and six months of consistently applying his method, the fits had completely stopped. This young woman, who had lived in constant fear of the next episode, found herself liberated from the grip of epilepsy, able to embrace life with newfound freedom and confidence.

Another extraordinary case involved a patient with a curvature of the spine. This individual had been attending Coué's clinic for four months, diligently practicing the method at home. To the astonishment of the patient's doctor, the spine was gradually resuming its normal position, which had previously seemed impossible without surgical intervention.

As word of Coué's success spread, people from across France and Europe sought his help. His conscious autosuggestion method achieved results that traditional medicine struggled to explain. Coué's work laid the foundation for our modern understanding of the power of positive thinking and affirmations, demonstrating our thoughts and beliefs' profound impact on our reality—a principle that now lies at the heart of manifestation.

Perhaps one of the most famous examples of the use of affirmations is by Muhammad Ali, widely regarded as one of the greatest boxers of all time. Long before he held any titles, when he was still known as Cassius Clay, Ali would confidently affirm, "I am the greatest!" He repeated this affirmation consistently, even when the boxing world doubted him. This unwavering belief in himself, reinforced through constant affirmation, played a crucial role in his journey to becoming a three-time world heavyweight champion and one of the most iconic athletes in history.

Ali once said, "It's the repetition of affirmations that leads to belief. And once that belief becomes a deep conviction, things begin to happen." This insight echoes Coué's emphasis on repetition and speaks to the power of consistently affirming our desired reality.

From Coué's pharmacy to Ali's boxing ring, the principle remains the same: our thoughts and beliefs shape our reality. But how can we use affirmations in our normal working lives every day? How do we create affirmations that resonate and align with our desires, and how can we use them to effectively manifest the life we want?

Why Affirmations Are Crucial in Manifestation

When I first started posting on social media, I dreamed of becoming globally recognized in the field of manifestation. I knew it in my heart but doubted it in my mind, so I deliberately chose to affirm: "I am a globally recognized manifestation coach, influencing lives daily." Initially, this felt wooden, and I remember my analytical mind almost laughing as I wrote down the affirmation. But I wanted to prove it wrong. It felt like a chore for the first few months and had not yet become subconsciously programmed. But I knew that if I persisted, the pen would eventually write the affirmation itself. As expected, like magic, around sixty days in, that's precisely what happened.

Within two months of starting posting regularly on Instagram, repeating this affirmation daily, and using all the other manifestation tools discussed in this book, I grew from less than one thousand followers to more than one hundred thousand.

To this day, I still use this specific affirmation, and now, with a global following, the affirmation has done its job beautifully. In fact, I experienced this kind of recognition during an ordinary shopping trip at my local supermarket, just before sitting down to write this section of the book. A man approached me and gently tapped on my shoulder. As I turned, he said, "Matt, you don't know me, but I wanted to say thank you. I follow you on Instagram, and your content has been helping me so much. I love what you do and just needed to thank you."

These encounters always touch me deeply. I set out with a dream to change lives, and when it happens, it's the best feeling in the world. Sometimes I have to remind myself that thousands of people see my posts, and that opens me up to recognition everywhere—supermarkets, restaurants, beaches, hotels, airports, and train stations. I never could have predicted this happening, and I'm sure it would have been a different story if I had consciously tried. But it was never my conscious mind's job to predict or determine how this would manifest. My job was to show up daily and plant the seed through frequent repetition.

My journey with affirmations highlights a crucial aspect of manifestation: the power of consciously chosen positive statements. However, it's essential to recognize that we're all using affirmations all the time, whether we realize it or not. The difference lies in whether these affirmations are consciously crafted to support our goals or unconsciously repeated patterns that may hold us back. To truly harness the power of affirmations, we need to understand both sides of this coin.

Throughout this book, we've been working toward a crucial goal: moving beyond wanting and stepping into the reality of being. Affirmations are not just a tool in this process; they're the bridge between your current state and the life you want to attract.

But here's an uncomfortable truth: most people who want to change their lives are affirming, day after day, the very reality they wish to escape. Thoughts like "I never have enough money," "Life is always hard," or "I'm not good enough" are what I call "unconscious affirmations." These aren't just negative thoughts; they're deeply ingrained beliefs we repeat to ourselves consistently, often without even realizing it.

When you repeat these statements daily, they become paradigms, or programs embedded in your subconscious mind. These paradigms form your belief system, and you accept them without conscious thought or analysis. They might not even be true, but they wire into your brain because you repeat them so often. Your subconscious lives in the landscape of the present moment and accepts whatever you feed it. It works tirelessly to make your beliefs a reality, whether positive or negative, taking orders from your conscious mind.

So if you think, "I am useless," your subconscious accepts this as truth. It then creates a biochemical response in your body, triggering emotions and actions that align with this belief.

This is why negative self-talk can be so damaging. Your subconscious doesn't distinguish between positive and negative statements. It simply acts on what it's told. Positive affirmations, on the other hand, are present-tense statements that we consciously repeat to ourselves with intention and belief. They are declarations of what we want to be true in our lives, expressed as if they are already our reality. These phrases are designed to challenge and overcome self-sabotaging and negative thoughts, replacing them with positive, empowering beliefs.

Our goal is to take our intentions—the reality we wish to create—and form them into bespoke, tailored affirmations, mantras, or statements. These are then expressed in the present tense and repeated consistently, reprogramming our subconscious mind. Just as unconscious affirmations can become deeply ingrained through constant repetition, the new, positive affirmations need the same level of consistency to take root. It's not about forcing yourself to believe something; it's about giving your mind a new truth to manifest. As you consistently affirm your desired reality, you begin to shift your subconscious beliefs. And as these new beliefs take hold, everything changes.

This process aligns with what Émile Coué discovered in his work: the power of repetition in programming the subconscious mind. The key is understanding that it's not your conscious mind doing the work. The intelligence that grows a baby from a single cell is the same intelligence that can heal the body or manifest your desires. But this intelligence exists beyond the analytical mind. You must transcend the conscious analytical mind to communicate with this powerful subconscious force, whether for healing, love, success, or abundance. You're giving it new instructions, new beliefs to manifest. And because your subconscious is always listening and accepting what you feed it, these new statements, instructions, and beliefs start shaping your reality by communicating directly with Universal intelligence.

How to Create Affirmations

When crafting affirmations, it's crucial to understand that our chosen words carry different energetic frequencies. By now, you'll know that we *never* use the phrase "I want" in our affirmations because this keeps us in a state of wanting rather than being. Instead, use words that convey the energy that moves you beyond wanting.

Let's examine how we can elevate our affirmations, from wanting to being, using wealth as an example:

"I want wealth" (lowest frequency) → "I feel wealthy" → "I receive wealth" → "I love wealth" → "I speak wealth into existence" → "I see wealth and abundance all around me" → "I am wealthy" (highest frequency)

This progression demonstrates how we can raise our affirmations to the purest state of being, which is "I am." These two simple words carry immense power. When you say, "I am," you're not just describing a temporary state or action; you're declaring your identity, your essence, and your present state of being. You're defining who you are at your core, which is the foundation for true manifestation.

Affirmations should feel true, even if they're not yet manifested in the physical world. Let's explore this concept through an example of a hardworking woman on the cusp of a life-changing venture. Consider Luna, a thirty-eight-year-old single mother of two working as a nurse in Chicago. For years, she's dreamed of creating a revolutionary pain-management device that combines aromatherapy with gentle vibration, inspired by her experiences with patients. Despite her passion, Luna's mind is clouded with doubts: "How can I find the time to do this?" "What if I fail?" "What if no one believes in my idea?" "How can I juggle my job, kids, and a start-up?" Luna's dreams are big: financial freedom, helping millions of people manage their pain, creating a legacy for her children, and finally having the time to travel and enjoy life. But her current reality feels far from these aspirations.

This is where the power of carefully crafted affirmations comes in. Luna needs to bridge the gap between her current state and her desired reality, starting with believable and inspiring affirmations. Initially, Luna might struggle with an affirmation like "I am a successful entrepreneur with a million-dollar company." It feels too far from her current reality. Instead, she could start with something like this:

"Every day, in every way, I am moving closer to bringing my pain-management device to those who need it most."

This affirmation acknowledges her journey while affirming her progress. As Luna becomes more comfortable, she can evolve her affirmations:

"I am open and ready to receive the financial investment and support I need to scale my marketing."

"I am balancing my roles as a nurse, mother, and entrepreneur with ease and flow."

"I am confidently attracting new customers with so much ease."

As Luna starts to manifest success, her affirmations can grow bolder:

"I am a successful entrepreneur, positively impacting thousands of lives with my innovative pain-management solution."

"I am financially free, with a beautiful million-dollar company."

Remember, believability is key, but that doesn't mean you can't dream big. When I first affirmed global recognition for my work, my logical mind scoffed. But a part of me knew that in today's world, all it takes is one viral video, one big break. The same applies to Luna. Although her analytical mind might doubt, a part of her sees the possibility. That's the part she's nurturing with these affirmations.

Think about what feels true for you. If your dream is big but you don't doubt yourself and the idea of writing the affirmation excites you, go for it. Don't hold back. However, suppose every part of you resists the affirmation because it feels so far out and as a result, you fear it will become an obstacle and potentially stop you from being consistent; then there's no problem reverse engineering it. As discussed in previous chapters, take your larger intent and create a smaller aspect to affirm.

The power lies in consistency and belief. If affirming "I am a millionaire" feels too far-fetched and makes you uncomfortable, start with "I am open to now receiving financial resources to aid my journey to freedom" or "Every day, I'm now taking steps toward financial freedom."

Affirmations should challenge you but not paralyze you. Find that sweet spot where they stretch your current reality but still resonate with your inner truth. This is where the real magic happens and where your subconscious mind begins to align with your deepest desires.

Keep your affirmations concise. Aim for one sentence, or two at the most. You want to be able to repeat them easily throughout the day. And consider using action words to make them more dynamic. "I am constantly attracting new opportunities for my business" feels more active and influential than "I attract new opportunities."

This approach to creating and evolving affirmations can be applied to any goal or dream. The process remains the same: identify your desires, address your fears, and craft positive, present-tense statements that resonate with your deepest aspirations. Remember, you're not just repeating words; you're reshaping your reality from the inside out, one affirmation at a time.

How to Use Affirmations

Incorporating affirmations into your daily routine doesn't require dramatic, mirror-chanting sessions. These powerful statements can be written or spoken, and their effectiveness lies in consistent, mindful repetition.

The subconscious mind is most receptive during the transitions between sleep and wakefulness, when our brain waves naturally slow down. This makes mornings and evenings ideal times for your affirmation practice. I integrate affirmations into my morning ritual, following my meditation, journaling, and gratitude exercises. It's the final step in my morning practice before I plug myself in to the outside world. I find power in putting pen to paper, so I write my affirmations in my notebook—they're always on the third page. You should feel free to do them at night if that better suits your schedule.

Another effective method is to use affirmations while you sleep. Some of my clients like to record themselves repeating their affirmations, add trance-inducing or soft background music, and play them on a loop for several hours while they sleep. This technique capitalizes on the brain's journey through various brain states:

1. Beta: Our normal waking, analytical state
2. Alpha: The first level of the subconscious, experienced as we begin to relax
3. Theta: A deeper subconscious state, associated with meditation and light sleep
4. Delta: Our deepest sleep state, during which the conscious mind is fully disengaged

As the affirmations play through headphones, they bypass the conscious mind's filters and directly imprint on the subconscious.

The key to a successful affirmation practice is finding a method that resonates with you, so experiment to see what's the best fit. Whether you're writing in a journal, speaking aloud, or listening while sleeping, your commitment to the practice is what will drive results.

The 369 Method

Nikola Tesla, the brilliant inventor who gave us alternating current electricity, was known for his peculiar obsessions. One of the most intriguing was his fascination with the numbers three, six, and nine. Tesla is alleged to have stated, "If you only knew the magnificence of the three, six, and nine, then you would have a key to the universe." Now, there's no definitive proof that Tesla actually said this. But the idea itself is interesting, and it aligns with many of Tesla's other known behaviors and beliefs. For instance, if you start doubling numbers (one, two, four, eight, sixteen, thirty-two, sixty-four), you'll notice that three, six, and nine are conspicuously absent from this pattern. Scientist Marko Rodin believes that three, six, and nine represent a "flux field," or a vector from the third to the fourth dimension. This might sound like science fiction, but it's an intriguing concept that makes you wonder about the hidden properties of these numbers.

Threes appear often in human history and culture. Think about it: triangles have three sides, as do pyramids. Trinities are present in religious and mythological traditions, such as the "Father, Son, and Holy Ghost" in Christianity. Tesla himself emphasized the importance of the three key concepts of energy, frequency, and vibration when he was quoted stating, "If you want to find the secrets of the universe, think in terms of energy, frequency and vibration." At the end of his life, Tesla was bouncing between cheap hotels and died in room number 3327 on the thirty-third floor of The New Yorker Hotel in January 1943. If you add the room number digits together (3 + 3 + 2 + 7), you get 15, which further reduces to 6 (1 + 5). It's as if these numbers followed him to the very end.

I was intrigued by all of this. I understood that these patterns show up in various ways in our world. For example, I was fascinated to learn that an atom is more than 99.99 percent empty space, with the rest consisting of energy and subatomic particles—another example of nature's precise mathematical patterns. These numerical patterns appear everywhere, even in our daily timekeeping: our familiar clock face divides neatly into these numbers: twelve (which reduces to three), quarter past (three on the clock face), half past (six on the clock face), and quarter to (nine on the clock face).

The recurring nature of these numbers made me wonder: Could they somehow enhance my manifestation game? I decided to test this by creating my own pattern of affirmations based on the 369 concept. Then, I committed to this practice for sixty-six days—another interesting number pattern that we've discussed in relation to habit formation.

The traditional 369 method of using affirmations involves writing your affirmation three times in the morning, six times in the afternoon, and nine times in the evening. This approach can be effective due to its emphasis on repetition, but I found it disruptive to stop in the middle of the day to write affirmations. It sometimes felt more like a chore, especially when I was enjoying time with my family on a Saturday afternoon.

My goal with reprogramming the subconscious mind is repetition and consistency, so I created my own bespoke way of doing it. Here's how it works:

1. **Create three affirmations of any length:** These should encompass your overall intent, such as your current dream or manifestation goal.

2. **Create one affirmation with exactly six words:** This is a concise statement that highlights an important aspect of your desires or what you feel would enhance your life. It doesn't need to sum up everything, just one meaningful part.

3. **Create one affirmation with exactly nine words:** Use this longer affirmation to paint a fuller picture of what you're aiming to achieve, incorporating various elements of your intentions.

Although my method incorporates five affirmations, the 369 pattern remains evident. In my view, this sequence captures the essence of these numbers and reflects the synchronized patterns that are significant.

To give you an example, here are the affirmations I used at the start of 2023:

Three affirmations:

"I am a globally recognized manifestation coach, influencing lives daily."

"I am an expert in my field, admired by many."

"Every day, in every way, fun and exciting opportunities come my way."

Six words:

"Money naturally flows with incredible ease."

Nine words:

"I am an influential voice attracting new clients effortlessly."

In this set, the three affirmations cover my overall intentions for recognition, expertise, and opportunities. The six-word affirmation addresses financial abundance, an area I wanted to improve. The nine-word affirmation encapsulates my overarching goal of becoming an influential voice and growing my client base.

After creating your affirmations, write them out like this:

Three:

[First affirmation of any length]

[Second affirmation of any length]

[Third affirmation of any length]

Six:

[Your six-word affirmation]

Nine:

[Your nine-word affirmation]

Once I have them written, I say these affirmations out loud three times. That's it. I don't go back to them at any other time during the day. I repeat this process every day and only change the affirmations when specific manifestations materialize or when I need to evolve them, typically after sixty-six days.

Here's an example using love as the main intention to manifest:

Three:

"I am worthy of deep, unconditional love and respect."

"My heart is open to giving and receiving love freely."

"I attract my perfect partner, who complements and supports me."

Six:

"Love flows abundantly in my life."

Nine:

"I am in a passionate relationship with my soulmate."

Remember, the key is consistency and belief in your affirmations. This method allows you to cover various aspects of your desire while maintaining the 369 pattern.

Whether Tesla's obsession with three, six, and nine truly

holds the key to the Universe or not, I've found that structuring affirmations this way creates a powerful framework for manifestation. It combines the mystical appeal of these numbers with practical, consistent application. Give it a try. You might just find that this numerical pattern unlocks new possibilities in your manifestation practice.

PRACTICE:

Creating Your Own Affirmations

Now that you've learned about the power of affirmations and various methods for using them, it's time to create your own practice. This five-step process will help you establish a robust, personalized affirmation ritual.

Step 1: Reflect and Set

Revisit your vision from chapter 4. If you could manifest anything from your twelve-month vision in the next two months, what would it be? It doesn't always have to be material. It could be a theme in your life, such as feeling more confident. Can you reverse engineer your twelve-month vision? Take your time with this step; clarity is crucial for crafting effective affirmations.

Step 2: Craft Your Affirmations

Create three affirmations that cover your overall intent, such as your current dream or manifestation goal.

Craft one affirmation that's exactly six words long. This is a concise statement that highlights an important aspect of your manifestation or what you feel would improve your life.

Develop one affirmation with exactly nine words that encapsulate your overarching goal. Remember to use present tense and positive language, and make them personal.

Step 3: Test-Drive (Seven Days)

Spend a week experimenting with your affirmations. Write them out every morning as part of your routine. Pay attention to how they feel. Do they resonate? Does saying them excite you? Try them at different times of the day and in various ways. You might practice them in the morning or evening, repeat them aloud, write them down, or record them and listen back to them. Follow your intuition, and don't hesitate to refine your affirmations if something doesn't feel right.

Step 4: Choose Your Method

Based on your test-drive, decide how to incorporate affirmations into your routine. Will you write them down each morning? Write them down each evening? Record them to listen to while you sleep? Use a combination of all these methods?

Step 5: Maintain Accountability and Long-Term Commitment

Use your accountability planner, and integrate your affirmations into your daily manifestation routine. Commit to your affirmation practice for at least sixty-six days. Mark your start date, and track your progress. Consistency is key. Make it a nonnegotiable part of your day. If you achieve your manifestation before the sixty-six days are up, or if you feel a strong urge to change your affirmations, revise them. The key is to maintain the practice, even as your goals evolve.

Remember, this is your unique journey. Don't rush the process of creating your affirmations. You want to ensure that you are happy with them. The goal is consistency, excitement, and belief. If you miss a day, don't beat yourself up—just pick up where you left off. Stick with it, even when it feels challenging or you are triggered by something external that might question or challenge your abilities. The results may not be immediate, but over time, you'll notice shifts in your mindset, your actions, and, eventually, your circumstances. This is how real, lasting change happens—one affirmation at a time, one day at a time.

CHAPTER 11

Let Go

When I finished the proposal for this book you're reading and my mentor, David, had gone through it with a fine-tooth comb, we were ready to pitch it to agents. There was one book that had been foundational for me during the summer of 2019 as I was developing my manifestation practice: *Atomic Habits* by James Clear. Its structure, style, and global impact was everything I wanted for my own book. David and I mused, "Wouldn't it be incredible to manifest the agent who helped James Clear?"

We pitched our proposal to James Clear's agent, and I held that intention during my meditations. A few days later, we got a polite rejection email. I was gutted. You know those moments when it feels like all of your hard work just crumbles? That's what it felt like. I was convinced this agent would be the one to help take *Beyond Wanting* to the market, but it wasn't meant to be.

Whenever I face rejection, one mantra has saved me time and again: "Rejection is protection." I first heard Gabby Bernstein say it, and it stuck. When we're rejected, we've got a choice. We can let it trigger us and bring us down, or we can catch it, reframe it, and see it as protection. What if that rejection is saving us from something that's not right for us? What if it's pushing us toward something even better that we can't see yet?

So David and I regrouped and pitched the book to nine more agents. In no time, I connected with Steve, an incredible agent from New York with a wealth of experience who also loved manifestation. It was a perfect match.

But the Universe wasn't done surprising me yet. Steve pitched to several publishing houses, including Penguin. When I got on a Zoom call with two Penguin editors, I noticed something mind-blowing: on one editor's bookshelf was a copy of *Atomic Habits*. It turned out that she was the editor who had helped James shape that very book.

I was stunned. I had set out to work with the agent of *Atomic Habits*, and the Universe delivered something even better—the very editorial department that had brought the book to life. Talk about a plot twist!

I couldn't have predicted or controlled this outcome. By staying open and not resisting when things didn't go as planned, I allowed the Universe to work its magic in ways far beyond what I could have imagined.

This is what letting go truly means in manifestation. It's about doing the work—visualizing, practicing gratitude, journaling, and all the other techniques we've discussed—and then remaining open and receptive. It's about trusting that what you seek is already coming to you. Your job is to keep that channel open, stay in vibrational alignment, and be ready to recognize and act on the signs when they appear.

It's not about sitting back and doing nothing. You're still actively engaged in the process, taking aligned, inspired action when it feels right. But you're not forcing it or obsessing over every detail. You're cocreating with the Universe, allowing it to bring your desire to you in the best way possible, which might be even better than you initially imagined.

Letting go means understanding that things might manifest in a way that's completely different from how you think they will. I wanted the agent and got the entire publishing powerhouse—a team of editors, designers, marketers, publicists, sales professionals, and production experts all working together to bring this book to life. The Universe heard and understood my intention but beautifully worked out a perfect match I couldn't have foreseen. If I hadn't stayed open and trusted by letting go of what I thought I wanted, I could have sabotaged my own manifestation.

So if what you wanted to manifest has yet to happen, or if you've faced rejection, ask yourself: "What if something even better is already on its way? What if the Universe is orchestrating something far more amazing than I could even imagine?"

When I started my manifestation journey, the idea of "letting go" left me feeling confused. I thought, "If I'm trying to manifest something, shouldn't I focus on it constantly? How can I let go and still make it happen?" Here's the thing: Letting go isn't about giving up—it's the complete opposite. Letting go is letting in.

Letting go is about trust and surrender. It's holding your vision clearly in your mind, feeling the emotions of already having what you desire, and then . . . releasing your grip on the how and when it will manifest.

But how do we practice the art of letting go? It all starts with understanding the power of nonresistance.

The Essence of Nonresistance

Letting go goes against everything we're used to. We've been told that to be successful, we must work hard for it, put in all the hours, fight, force, stay up late, put in overtime, meticulously plan, and worry if things don't happen when we think they should. But that very way of being creates resistance. It keeps you separate from what you want. Pushing and forcing create resistance, not resonance.

Nonresistance is about not resisting the urge to get in the way of your own creation and manage it into existence. If you do this, it's not really manifestation; it's manufacturing it into reality. Letting go and surrendering control move you beyond wanting and into resonance—a subtle but significant shift that aligns you with the vibrational frequency of your desire.

When our manifestations don't appear as quickly as we'd like, it's easy to slip into fear, stress, or worry. We start doubting and forcing, creating the exact opposite of reception—we create resistance. Resistance is like a barrier between you and your desires. It's the energy of lack, of not having, of struggle.

When you're in resistance, you're vibrating at a frequency that doesn't match what you want to attract. If you're feeling frustrated, not seeing signs, or tired of pushing against what feels immovable, try something different. Take a deep breath. Loosen your grip. Continue connecting with your vision daily, but do so from a place of trust and gratitude rather than from lack or desperation.

In a state of nonresistance, you become receptive to guidance, synchronicities, and opportunities you might have missed when you were forcing your own agenda. Think about times when things flowed effortlessly in your life. Chances are, you weren't trying so hard. You were simply being, allowing life to unfold naturally.

To truly understand the power of nonresistance, let's look at a remarkable real-life example. In 1974, actor Anthony Hopkins was at a crossroads. His career was faltering, and he was eager for a breakthrough role. When offered a chance to audition for *The Girl from Petrovka*, Hopkins set out to find a copy of the book on which the film was based. He scoured every bookshop in London, growing increasingly frustrated with each failed attempt. Eventually, exhausted and disheartened, he let go of his search. Later that day, while waiting for a train at Leicester Square Station, Hopkins noticed an abandoned bound manuscript on a nearby bench. To his astonishment, it was a copy of *The Girl from Petrovka*, complete with the author's notes.

A year later, Hopkins met the author, George Feifer, while filming in Vienna. Amazingly, he learned that this was Feifer's lost copy, which he had misplaced while working in London. In that moment of surrender, the Universe had delivered exactly what Hopkins needed, in a way he could never have anticipated.

But how do we put this into practice? How can we learn to trust in something we can't see or control? This is where we need to dive deeper into trusting the unknown and facing our fears head-on.

Trusting in the Unknown

When we truly let go in manifestation, we're confronted with the vast expanse of the unknown. I've been there, and I know it can be unsettling. It challenges our very perception of reality and control. That's exactly how it feels when we let go—our inner animal screams, and the ego built on being in control rebels. It's our job to battle that ego and trust in something else, the unknown.

As humans, we perceive about 0.0035 percent of the entire electromagnetic spectrum with our naked eye. That's like wearing a highly restrictive virtual reality headset. We're seeing only a fraction of what truly exists. Now imagine removing that headset. Suddenly, the world expands exponentially. What we thought was empty space is teeming with energy and possibility. This leads to a question I want you to consider: What would you rather trust—the "knowns," that tiny fraction of reality, or the "unknown," that invisible 99.9965 percent of reality invisible to the human eye?

Our struggle with trusting the unknown stems from our deeply ingrained survival instincts. We're wired to fear what we can't see or understand because, historically, the unknown could pose a threat to our survival. This instinct, although once crucial, now can hold us back from embracing the vast potential of the Universe.

We often fear the unknown because we can't control it. We're afraid of uncertainty and things not working out as planned. But what if the unknown isn't something to be feared, but rather an infinite field of possibilities waiting to be explored? What if our limited perception is preventing us from seeing the miraculous ways the Universe can bring our desires to fruition?

Trusting the unknown requires a paradigm shift. It's about recognizing that our conscious minds, amazing as they are, are limited in their capacity to understand and control the complex workings of the Universe. By trusting in the unknown, we're not giving up control—we're tapping into a higher intelligence that can orchestrate events in ways far beyond our imagination.

At the core of this struggle with the unknown lies our ego (not in the sense of being egotistical, but as a complex part of our psyche shaped by our unique life experiences). Think of the ego as your inner bodyguard, always on alert, interpreting the world through the lens of your past to keep you safe. This protective instinct is valuable in many situations, but it can become a significant obstacle in your manifestation journey.

Your ego's influence might show up differently in your life. You may have developed a strong need for control, making it challenging to let go and trust the manifestation process. Or maybe past disappointments have led your ego to be overly cautious, holding you back from fully committing to your desires.

In our world of instant gratification, where we can order a meal, book a ride, or start a movie with a single tap, our egos have adapted to expect immediate results. But manifestation often unfolds in ways that defy this now-or-never mentality. It's more like planting a garden than ordering takeout. You plant the seeds (set your intentions), nurture them (align your energy), and then trust in the unseen growth happening beneath the surface. If it's not your ego holding you back, it's often its close companion, fear.

Like the ego, fear can be both a protector and an obstacle. Some fears are genuine and serve a vital purpose. If you're being chased by a lion, fear triggers a life-saving response, prompting you to run with all your might. However, when it comes to manifestation, our fears are rarely as tangible or immediate.

When fear arises in your journey, pause and ask yourself: "Is this fear based on a real threat, or is it a product of my imagination? What am I truly afraid of? Is it the possibility that my manifestation won't happen on my timeline? What if my desire is already manifesting but I haven't recognized it yet? Or what if the Universe is preparing something even better than I could imagine?"

Our brains are like record players, constantly replaying past experiences in an attempt to predict the future. When reality doesn't match these predictions, our brain perceives it as a potential threat. This is where FEAR (false evidence appearing real) often comes from. If you can't physically see or touch the source of your fear, it's worth questioning whether it's a genuine threat or a creation of your mind.

In my own journey, every time I've chosen to trust the unknown despite my fears, it has never let me down. The outcomes often have been far better than anything I could have planned. If you've been practicing letting go but still struggle to see results, consider simplifying your approach. When we fixate on manifesting the end result, we're essentially trying to manifest a massive amount of energy all at once. Instead, focus on the next small step. This requires less energy and makes it easier to trust the process and let go.

Remember, the Universe doesn't operate on our concept of linear time—in the quantum field, everything is happening now. The energy of your desire is being orchestrated behind the scenes, but it will only manifest when your energy aligns perfectly with it. In our three-dimensional reality, this alignment process appears as the passage of time, which can be frustrating. We think, "It's taking so long," or "I'm not seeing any signs." This is precisely why letting go is crucial. It allows this natural unfolding to occur without the interference of our impatience or doubt.

When I feel the fear of letting go creeping in, I don't retreat. Instead, I lean in further. I take a deep breath and affirm: "I trust in the infinite wisdom of the unknown. I'm open to the Universe surprising and delighting me in unexpected ways." So the next time fear arises around letting go, remind yourself: this isn't about relinquishing control; it's about cocreating with a Universe with infinitely more resources and possibilities than your limited human perspective can fathom.

PRACTICE:

Seven-Day Let Go Challenge

This practice is designed to help you gently challenge your ego's need for control and cultivate trust in the Universal flow. Start with something small but significant.

Step 1: Identify Your Grip

Choose one small habit or behavior representing your ego's need for control. Take a moment to reflect on your current personality. What are you holding onto tightly? Some relatable examples might be the following:

- Constantly checking your phone for a message from someone you're trying to manifest a relationship with
- A timeline you're adamant about
- Constantly checking for signs or synchronicities
- Refreshing your email repeatedly, hoping for news about a job interview or other opportunity

Step 2: Understand the Root

Now, dig deeper. Why are you holding on to this so tightly? Is it because of past experiences? Fear of the unknown? A belief that if you don't control it, it won't happen? Try to trace this back to its origin.

Step 3: Set Your Intention

In your journal, write down: "During the next seven days, I am open and ready to let go of [enter your chosen manifestation grip] and deeply trust in the divine timing of my manifestation. I choose to release control and allow the Universe to surprise me in ways I couldn't have imagined."

Step 4: The Seven-Day Complete Release

Commit to completely letting go of your chosen behavior for the next week. This isn't about setting specific times or limiting yourself; it's about fully releasing control. Here's how to approach different scenarios:

If you've been constantly checking your phone for a message from someone specific, keep your phone with you but consciously resist the urge to check it for that particular person. When you feel the impulse, take a deep breath and remind yourself, "What's meant for me will not pass me by." Focus on engaging fully with your surroundings or the task at hand instead.

If you've been refreshing your email for job news, keep your email accessible, but set a conscious intention to check it only when necessary for your daily tasks. When you feel the urge to refresh for that specific news, pause and say to yourself, "The right opportunity will find me at the perfect time."

If you've been overusing dating apps, take a seven-day break from them. If it helps, temporarily uninstall them. Use the time you would have spent swiping to engage in self-care activities, pursue hobbies, or connect with friends and family. Trust that the right person will come into your life at the right time, with or without the apps.

Step 5: Weekly Review
At the end of the seven days, review and ask yourself the following:

- What did I learn from this experience about my manifestation journey?
- How has my relationship with control and trust shifted?
- If I felt resistance, where did it come from?

- Did I notice any synchronicities, signs, or anything else unexpected?
- How can I apply this letting-go mindset to other aspects of my manifestation practice?

As you practice letting go, you will likely notice an exciting shift. The world around you may feel more alive with meaning. You might catch yourself thinking, "What are the odds?" more often. That song lyric that perfectly captures your situation, the recurring number that catches your eye, or that chance encounter that opens new possibilities—these aren't just random events.

These signs and synchronicities often become more noticeable when we release our need for control. It's like tuning in to a frequency you didn't know existed before. In the next chapter, we'll explore how to spot these signs, understand their significance, and use them to navigate your manifestation journey. For now, as you let go, stay aware. Notice the little coincidences and unexpected alignments. They're often the Universe's way of confirming you're on the right path.

Remember, letting go isn't just about releasing control; it's about opening yourself up to guidance. Letting go is letting in. So embrace this challenge, and get ready to see your world through new eyes. The signs are there. Are you ready to see them?

CHAPTER 12

Signs

The Universe finally gave us a clear sign. Our dream of moving to Cornwall began to materialize when a house that seemed tailor-made for us appeared on the market. It wasn't just any property; it was exactly what we'd been manifesting. Picture this: a charming four-bedroom detached cottage nestled in a picturesque Cornish village, brimming with character, and surrounded by beautiful gardens. It even had the potential for an annex, perfect for Corisande's parents to join us.

But there was a catch. It was 20 percent over our budget. We didn't let that stop us though. We arranged a viewing and, as expected, fell in love with the place. At this point, my ego kicked into overdrive. It was frantically trying to calculate how we could scrape together the extra 20 percent needed for the house. To put this in perspective, we're talking about a sum larger than the entire value of our first house.

I had absolutely no doubt about my ability to manifest this

money. That wasn't the issue. The real challenge was the timeline I was up against. Houses in Cornwall tend to fly off the market, especially in this village, and I knew that this narrow window of time was creating a weak energetic alignment. I couldn't shake the sense of urgency and was acutely aware that it was interfering with my manifestation process. This urgency was breeding disbelief, and I knew that was a recipe for misalignment.

So what did I do? First, I needed to be honest with myself. I took a step back and checked in with how I was truly feeling—a practice I use to assess my emotional state and energy. I sat quietly, took a few deep breaths, and noticed what was happening in my body and mind. Sure enough, I could feel that wanting energy taking over. As you now understand, this pushed me farther out of alignment. This moment brought all my years of manifestation practice into focus. I knew that to have any chance of buying this house, I needed to let go.

As we covered in the previous chapter, letting go means letting in. It's one of the most challenging aspects of manifestation, seeing what looks like your perfect desire right in front of you yet just out of reach. The key was to remain open and receptive rather than feeling a sense of need or want.

In a situation like this, the best approach is to seek guidance and ask for a sign. I turned to a technique I learned from José Silva's book *The Silva Mind Control Method*. Before bed one night, I visualized our situation: the perfect house, just beyond our current means. I imagined handing this scenario to my higher self and asking for guidance. In my journal, I wrote: "Tonight, I will remember my dreams. I'm open and ready to receive a sign or guidance about our move to Cornwall." This wasn't about giving up. It was about tuning in. By stepping back from the stress of trying to force a solution, I opened myself up to receive guidance. I trusted that the Universe would provide the answers I needed.

That night, I experienced one of the most vivid dreams I've ever had. I woke up with my heart racing, every detail of my dream clearly etched in my mind. In it, Corisande, her parents, and I were viewing an incredible farmhouse. We were walking around with a real estate agent, and I felt excited as we took in the features—exposed beams, wood-burning stoves, and sprawling gardens. The house was located next to a farm, with outbuildings nearby. In the dream, I remember thinking, "This place is perfect. How is it still available?" Then came the twist. The agent turned to me and said, "If you want it, it's available to rent."

I woke up with a mix of emotions. I had this exciting dream about a house, only to be told it wasn't even for sale. I immediately wrote down all the details, curious about what this might mean. It struck me that instead of showing me the house we wanted to buy, the Universe had presented us with something entirely different: a home available to rent. Sometimes signs don't align perfectly with our expectations or desires. Instead, they offer guidance that may initially seem puzzling or even contradictory. The key is to remain open to the message, even if it's not what we anticipated, and trust the intelligence of the sign rather than our limited conscious mind.

Later that day, Corisande and I went shopping at Bicester Village in Oxfordshire. Over breakfast, I shared my dream with her. Corisande was skeptical about renting—she'd been set on buying a house for two years, and this potential shift in plans didn't sit well with her. As a manifestation coach, I had to remind myself (and her) that the path to our desires isn't always straightforward; sometimes we have to follow the twists and turns.

On a hunch, I pulled out my phone and opened Rightmove, a UK property search app. To my amazement, there it was—the exact house I'd described in my dream, available to rent in a fantastic location we knew well. Corisande was still hesitant. Renting instead of buying was a significant shift from our plan. As I explained to Corisande that maybe this was the Universe guiding us in a new direction, the bill arrived: £44.44. Right at that moment, I knew it was another sign.

Repeating number sequences like this carry messages, and with previous experience, I knew that the repetition of fours symbolized foundations and support. Corisande wasn't convinced, seeing it as a coincidence. But the Universe wasn't done with us yet. As we crossed the road and entered a shop, I noticed something intriguing about the saleswoman helping Corisande. Her necklace caught my eye, and I could make out a number on the pendant. When I asked her about it, she showed me. The necklace read "444." This was within fifteen minutes of seeing £44:44 on our bill across the street.

"What does that mean?" I asked.

"It's an angel number," she replied with a smile. "It means guidance, support, and foundations." Corisande and I were stunned. There's no other way to describe that moment.

The message was crystal clear: the Universe was guiding us toward renting. I didn't understand why, but I accepted that my conscious mind's comprehension is limited compared to Universal intelligence.

Despite our initial desire to buy the other house, we trusted this guidance. We decided to follow the signs and rent first. I knew we would eventually buy that house or something better. But I also understood that controlling the outcome wasn't my job. My role was simply to stay in flow and follow the signs the Universe was so clearly providing.

Trusting this guidance, we drove four hours to Cornwall the next day. It was a Sunday, meaning the real estate agents were closed, and we had yet to determine if the rental property was still available. But we felt compelled to take this leap of faith. This is what I call taking "aligned, inspired action," which I'll cover in detail in the next chapter. We acted on the signs and intuition we'd received, aligning our actions with the Universe's guidance.

I called the agent first thing Monday morning. Her response hit me like a bucket of cold water: "I'm sorry, but the property has been rented. The new tenants are due to get the keys on Thursday." I was shocked. It didn't make sense. All these signs pointed us toward renting the exact property from my dream, which now seemed out of reach. So there we were, our dream house 20 percent out of budget and the perfect rental slipping through our fingers.

"What are you playing at, Universe?" I thought, trying to keep my emotions in check. It was hard not to feel triggered, but we had no choice but to drive back home, confused and disheartened. Two days crawled by. Then, on Wednesday, my phone rang. It was the agent from Cornwall.

"Hi, Matt. I was wondering whether you're still interested in the property you inquired about on Monday."

Surprised, I replied, "Yes, I am."

"Well," she continued, "I'm calling because the lady who was supposed to pick up the keys tomorrow has changed her mind. The property's available again."

I could feel the energy shift as she spoke. The Universe wasn't done with us yet.

"There were other people on the waiting list," the agent added, "but none have returned my calls or picked up. You're the first person I've spoken to. Are you interested?"

"Absolutely," I said without hesitation.

Her next words resonated deeply: "Sometimes in life, these things are meant to be, aren't they? If you want it, it's yours." Those words stuck with me. It was as if the Universe had orchestrated this entire sequence of events, testing our faith and alignment before delivering precisely what we needed.

The next day, Corisande and her parents journeyed back to Cornwall. I was tied up with coaching clients, so I joined them via FaceTime as they viewed the property. I felt a surreal sense of déjà vu as they walked through each room. This was the exact house from my dream, materializing before our eyes. We didn't hesitate. We took it.

We picked up the keys two weeks later. Holding them in my hand, I marveled at how the Universe had brought us to this moment. From a vivid dream to an actual set of keys, our Cornwall adventure was truly beginning.

But the story doesn't end there. The Universe had more in store for us, revealing its uncanny ability to see the path ahead, even when it makes no sense to us in the present moment. The original dream house sold shortly after we moved into the rented accommodation. But rather than seeing this as a setback, I recognized it as part of the journey. In fact, our whole life exploded with growth as soon as we moved to Cornwall. Writing this book was part of that. There has been a whole new energy and vibration since we moved. And we wouldn't have experienced that energy or that vibration if we had just stayed in our previous location.

The ripple effect of this alignment continued. Our business exploded with new opportunities and success, and my social media following skyrocketed. But the most precious manifestation of all came a few months later. The new energy we'd tapped into helped us easily manifest our first pregnancy. It was as if the Universe was showering us with blessings, one after another.

So although we hadn't yet manifested a house to buy, we had manifested an entirely new state of being and energy, which was taking our life to a new level. Another four months later, not only did the house we'd initially wanted unexpectedly come back on the market, but another property also appeared that surpassed our dreams.

This new house was in the same village, five fields away from the first one. It had four bedrooms, an attached annex, beautiful character features, and lovely gardens. The gardens weren't quite as large as at the other house, but here's the kicker: it was 20 percent less in value, exactly matching the budget Corisande and I had initially set to the penny!

I was amazed at how this journey had unfolded. Here we were, already living our best life in a beautiful rental property in Cornwall, with a thriving business and a growing family on the way, and only twelve months earlier, I'd set the intention to purchase a house with specific features, in a specific location, for a specific amount. The Universe had delivered, again, but in a way we couldn't have imagined.

The only difference—and this is crucial—was that it happened six months later than we'd initially hoped. But there's always divine timing at play. The Universe isn't working on our timeline. It hears our intentions, knows the path forward, and, in its wisdom, knew that renting first would allow us to establish our foundations in Cornwall and open us up to even more incredible blessings.

We are now the proud owners of our dream house, and what makes it even more remarkable is that when I started writing this book, this manifestation was still unfolding.

My journey mirrors the process I'm sharing with you, chapter by chapter.

The Power of Dreams

In my work as a manifestation coach, I've found dreams to be a potent tool for seeking guidance, especially when you're feeling stuck or unsure about your path. Dreams are unique because they occur when our analytical mind is at rest, allowing us to access deeper levels of consciousness. This shift in consciousness might be the key to why dreams are such powerful conduits for signs and guidance.

Think back to the PEAR experiments we discussed in chapter 5. Remember how the subconscious mind could more successfully influence physical reality? When we dream, we operate almost entirely from our subconscious. I believe this subconscious mind is in constant communication with the unified field of intelligence we've been exploring throughout this book. Without the noise of our waking thoughts, we're more open to receiving messages from this field.

It's important to note that not all dreams are filled with hidden messages or profound insights. Sometimes they're simply the brain's way of processing the day's events, moving information from short-term to long-term memory. But occasionally, you might experience something extraordinary—a "precognitive dream."

Precognition is when you're shown an exact future scenario before it unfolds in waking life. This isn't just déjà vu; it's a vivid dream that later plays out in reality, often with startling accuracy. These dreams suggest that some of us can access information beyond our current timeline. It's as if that aspect of ourselves that exists outside linear time is sending us a message, giving us a glimpse into potential future events.

If you're interested in harnessing your dreams to get a sign, here's a simple yet effective technique: when you're in bed, just before you're about to turn in for sleep, write in your journal three times, "Tonight, I'll remember my dreams." This act of intention-setting primes your subconscious to pay attention to your dreams. Then, first thing in the morning, as you're coming out of those slow brain waves, write down anything you remember, even if it's just one word, a face, or a person. Don't judge or analyze anything at this stage; simply record what comes to mind. I strongly recommend adding this practice to your daily accountability tracker. Consistency is key when working with dreams and signs.

The ability to remember dreams and receive signs through

them is like exercising a muscle—the more you work at it, the stronger your dream recall will become. Over time, you'll likely find your dreams becoming clearer and more vivid. You might start noticing patterns, recurring symbols, or even direct messages that relate to your waking life and manifestation goals.

Now let's translate this dreamwork to your broader manifestation practice. The same process of openness and receptivity applies when manifesting relationships, jobs, businesses, or anything else. What if there's someone even better suited for you than the person you currently think is "the one"? What if there's a career path that's an even better fit than the one you're currently pursuing? Our job is to follow the signs like breadcrumbs, staying open to possibilities we may not have initially considered.

Ask yourself: "Am I holding too tightly to one specific outcome? Am I open to the possibility that the Universe might have something better for me?" Remember, manifestation is a journey filled with twists and turns. If you stay balanced and calm, you'll realize that the Universe is working on your desires and you're just caught up in the middle of the process.

The key is to remain open, trust the process, and be willing to follow where the signs lead, even if it's not where you initially thought you were going. Your dream might unfold unexpectedly, but the Universe's plan often surpasses our imagination. Our story of manifesting our move to Cornwall is proof of that.

By incorporating dreamwork into your manifestation practice, you're opening up a powerful channel of communication with your subconscious and the Universe. It's another tool in your manifestation toolkit, one that can provide insights, guidance, and sometimes even glimpses of the future you're creating.

What Are Signs, and Where Do They Come From?

As we explored in chapter 1, quantum mechanics shows us that the observer affects reality at a subatomic level. This concept is critical to understanding where signs come from and how they manifest in our physical three-dimensional life. I believe signs originate from our deep interconnectedness with a unifying intelligence field—the quantum field. This infinite realm of potential contains every possibility as energy. Our thoughts and emotions, also forms of energy, constantly interact with this field, often without our conscious awareness.

I've come to understand signs as the unfolding of our manifestation. We often expect our desires to materialize instantly, but manifestation sometimes can be a gradual process of energy transitioning into physical form. Signs are the breadcrumbs of this transition, guiding us toward our manifestation.

Let's use the example of my house in Cornwall. A year before it materialized, the Universe heard my intentions. The energy required for that manifestation first appeared as signs: angel numbers, dreams, and the whole process of renting to eventually finding the perfect house. All of this was the manifestation unfolding.

When we open ourselves to receiving signs, we tap into this realm of pure potential. It's like fine-tuning our personal energy to resonate with specific frequencies in the quantum field. By setting an intention to receive a sign or staying present to spot it, we're like scientists observing quantum particles. Our act of observation causes the energy to collapse from a wave of potential into a particle of experience—a sign. These signs can manifest in various ways:

- Media messages (for example, a timely song on the radio)
- Animal encounters (like a robin appearing at a significant moment)
- Vivid or recurring dreams
- Recurring symbols (like repeatedly finding a white feather)
- Digital signs (relevant social media posts or emails)
- Angel numbers (repeating number sequences)
- Synchronistic events
- Sudden intuitive feelings
- Books opening to relevant pages
- Technology glitches with seeming messages
- Physical sensations (like goose bumps)

A part of us—our Higher Self or Oversoul—exists outside linear time, connected to a greater consciousness. This aspect can provide guidance from beyond our limited, time-bound perspective. When we receive signs, we're transforming potential energy into tangible reality through our awareness and guidance from this timeless part of ourselves. Consider a newborn baby instinctively seeking its mother's milk. There's no manual, no hard drive telling it what to do, no prior experience—just pure intuition. This baby is tapping into the same guidance system we all have but often learn to doubt as we grow. As adults, we still have this ability, but it's frequently drowned out by the noise of our experiences and fears.

While these signs exist, we always have free will. We can choose to follow the breadcrumbs or forge our own path. When I saw signs pointing me toward renting in Cornwall, I could have ignored them. But by trusting this guidance—even when it seemed illogical—I ended up where I needed to be.

Synchronicities are the Universe responding to your vibrational output, reflecting your inner world through tangible experiences. They're not just coincidences, but early indications that your manifestation is taking shape, like ripples on a pond signaling something more significant to come. We all can learn to spot and trust these signs. It's about rekindling that innate wisdom we had as newborns, leveraging our adult experiences, and opening ourselves to the potential around us while being willing to follow a path that might not always make sense to our logical minds.

Remember, just because you can't see something doesn't mean it doesn't exist. By staying open and aware, you'll start to notice the subtle ways the Universe is guiding you toward your desires, even before they fully materialize in your reality.

Understanding Angel Numbers

Have you ever experienced the uncanny phenomenon of repeating number sequences popping up everywhere—11:11 on clocks, 888 on license plates, or 333 in phone numbers? If you've dismissed these as mere coincidences, it might be time to reconsider. These recurring patterns, often referred to as angel numbers, could be carrying profound messages for you. Once you start paying attention, you'll likely notice these patterns appearing more frequently, as if they're trying to teach you something important about your journey.

Numbers carrying spiritual significance isn't a modern concept. It dates to ancient times, with roots in various cultures and philosophical traditions. Greek mathematician and philosopher Pythagoras introduced the belief that numbers possess unique vibrational energies. He famously proclaimed, "Numbers rule the universe," which laid the foundation for numerology, which offers a framework for understanding how these numerical sequences influence our lives.

While science provides us with a framework to understand the Universe, my personal beliefs and experiences have led me to a more expansive interpretation. I've come to view these numbers not just as symbols, but as "angles"—specific angles of light or energy. This perspective is inspired by concepts from modern physics, particularly string theory and M-theory, which suggest the existence of multiple dimensions beyond the three spatial and one temporal dimension we commonly experience. This multidimensional view aligns beautifully with the central principle of numerology: that the Universe and everything within it is fundamentally vibrational. Just as Pythagoras recognized the vibrational nature of numbers thousands of years ago, quantum physics has now revealed the vibrational nature of all matter and energy. We're not just living in a universe; we're part of a vibrating, multidimensional cosmos.

As multidimensional beings, I believe we're not limited to this three-dimensional existence. Those gut feelings, flashes of intuition, or predictive dreams you've experienced? They're not just random occurrences. They're hinting that part of us operates beyond conventional space and time, tapping into realms of existence we're only beginning to understand. In my view, these number synchronicities are significant messages, or "angles" of insight, provided by our multidimensional self. They're like cosmic guideposts designed to help us align more closely with our true path and highest potential. When we see these angel numbers, we're observing the intersection points where these higher dimensions touch our everyday reality. It's as if the Universe is leaving us breadcrumbs, guiding us toward our highest good.

Decoding Angel Numbers

You may be wondering what angel numbers mean when you see them and how you can use them effectively to help you on your manifestation journey. Here's my personal decoder for some common angel numbers. Remember, these are my interpretations based on years of research and personal experience. The key is to use them, reflect on how they resonate with you, and develop your own understanding over time.

000—Oneness and infinite potential: Zeros symbolize interconnectedness and the start of a spiritual journey. You might see this when you're facing major life changes or spiritual awakenings, or when you need to tap into your unlimited potential.

111—New beginnings and manifestation: Ones signal it's time to embrace new opportunities and manifest your thoughts. This often appears when you're considering career changes, when you're starting new projects, or when your thoughts are aligning with your reality.

222—Balance and partnerships: Twos emphasize harmony in relationships and life aspects. You might see this when you're dealing with conflicts, deciding about partnerships, or finding equilibrium in various areas of your life.

333—Expression and creativity: Threes encourage self-expression, creativity, and improved communication. This could appear when you need to share ideas, pursue creative endeavors, or enhance communication in your relationships.

444—Foundations, guidance, and protection: Fours suggest it's time to build stability and structure in your life, while also indicating divine guidance and protection. You might see this when you're making important decisions, seeking reassurance, or planning for your long-term future.

555—Change and freedom: Fives signal significant life changes and the need for personal freedom. This often appears when you're facing major transitions, need to break free from old patterns, or are ready to embrace new adventures.

666—Family and material balance: Sixes direct attention to domestic life, family relationships, and the need for balancing material concerns. You might see this when you need to focus more on home life, address family issues, or reassess your attachment to material possessions. It's a reminder to find harmony between your worldly responsibilities and spiritual growth.

777—Spiritual awakening and intuition: Sevens encourage spiritual growth, introspection, and trusting your inner wisdom. This could appear when you're exploring life's deeper questions, developing psychic abilities, or need to rely more on your intuition.

888—Abundance and personal power: Eights symbolize financial prosperity, success, and personal empowerment. You might encounter this when new opportunities for growth are emerging, or when you need to recognize your own power to create abundance.

999—Completion and universal love: Nines represent the end of a cycle, spiritual enlightenment, and humanitarianism. This often appears when you're concluding a significant life phase, are called to serve others, or need to let go of something to move forward.

Mixed numbers: When you encounter mixed number sequences, like 7:11 or 1234, consider the meanings of each number involved. For example, with 7:11, you might blend the spiritual insight of seven with the new beginnings of one. The key is to trust your intuition and consider how these combined energies might relate to your current situation.

When you see these numbers, immediately ask yourself: "What was I thinking about in that moment?" or "What's going on in my life right now?" This instant reflection can provide valuable context for interpreting the message.

I encourage you to keep these number interpretations handy. Jot them down in a notebook you carry with you or take a screenshot of this section. This way, you'll be able to quickly access their meanings whenever they appear in your life. As you become more attuned to angel numbers, you'll notice how they appear in meaningful contexts. For instance, if you're contemplating a career change and keep seeing 111, the Universe might be encouraging you to take that leap of faith. Or if you're struggling with work-life balance and 222 keeps appearing, the Universe could be prompting you to reassess your priorities.

To deepen your understanding, keep a journal of the numbers you see and the circumstances surrounding them. Note your thoughts, feelings, and any events that coincide with these numerical appearances. Over time, you'll develop your own nuanced interpretation of how these angelic messages apply to your life.

Remember, the interpretations provided here are just a starting point. Your personal experiences and intuition will guide you to a deeper, more personalized understanding of these numerical signs. As you continue this journey, you may wish to explore the many online resources and books available that delve deeper into the meanings of angel numbers. The Universe is always speaking to you through these numbers; all you need to do is listen.

PRACTICE:

Asking for Signs

As we conclude this chapter, I want to provide a practical exercise to apply what you've learned about signs and angel numbers. Remember, there's a specific way to ask for a sign. You can't force it or desperately want it—that creates resistance. Instead, you need to put yourself in a position to be open to receiving.

Here's how to do it:

Step 1: Identify Your Question

Think about an aspect of your life that feels out of your grip. It could be something you need help with, a challenge you're facing, or an area where manifestation seems slow despite your efforts. Clarity is essential here. The more specific you are, the clearer the guidance can be.

Step 2: Write Your Request

Get a pen and paper. Before you start your day in the morning, write: "I am now open and ready to receive guidance in the form of a sign to help me understand the path forward regarding [your specific issue]. I'm so grateful for this sign. Thank you, thank you, thank you." Repeat this exercise before bed for dream guidance, adding: "Tonight, I will remember my dreams. Tonight, I will remember my dreams. Tonight, I will remember my dreams."

Step 3: Sit with It
Take a few moments to sit quietly with your request. Feel the gratitude and openness in your body. Visualize yourself receiving clear guidance.

Step 4: Set and Forget
This is crucial. Completely let go of your request for at least forty-eight hours. Refrain from obsessing or hunting for signs. Trust that the Universe has heard you.

Step 5: Reflect and Observe
During the next forty-eight hours, cultivate a state of heightened awareness. Rather than actively searching for signs, allow yourself to be more present in each moment. This receptive state will make you naturally more attuned to the subtle whispers of the Universe.

Step 6: Repeat the Process
If you don't receive a clear sign within the first forty-eight hours, or if the sign doesn't make sense, don't worry. Repeat steps 2 through 5 every forty-eight hours. Consistency is key.

Step 7: Collect the Evidence
Act like an investigator. Keep a journal of any potential signs you notice. Write down dreams, number sequences, unusual occurrences—anything that stands out.

Step 8: Decode the Message

After a week of this practice, review your "evidence." Look for patterns or recurring themes. Trust your intuition as you interpret what these signs might mean about your initial question.

Step 9: Prepare for Aligned, Inspired Action

As you decode the Universe's messages, you may feel drawn to specific actions or decisions. This is where the true magic unfolds—but it's also where many falter. Acting on these signs is a delicate art that blends intuition, courage, and discernment.

In the next chapter, we'll explore step 9 in depth. You'll learn to translate the signs into tangible steps, distinguishing between fear-based reactions and genuinely inspired action. I'll guide you in moving forward confidently, even when the path ahead seems unclear.

For now, immerse yourself in the practice of receiving and interpreting signs. As you do, you'll become increasingly fluent in the Universe's subtle language. Each sign you notice, and each message you decode, is a step toward a more aligned, intentional life.

CHAPTER 13

Aligned, Inspired Action

Around the late 1990s, a young woman was having a particularly rough day selling fax machines door-to-door. People were literally ripping up her business cards in her face. Fed up, she pulled over and had a moment of clarity: "I'm in the wrong movie," she thought. "Call the director; call the producer. This is not my life. How did this happen?" That night, she went home and wrote in her journal, asking herself, "What am I good at?" The one thing in her "Good" column was sales. She dug deeper, questioning, "What is it about sales that I like?" She realized she enjoyed offering something to people that either improved their lives or fulfilled a need. With this insight, she wrote, "I want to invent a product that I can sell to millions of people that will make them feel good." Then, she did something crucial: she asked for an idea to come to her and patiently waited. This woman was Sara Blakely, and that moment of frustration became the catalyst for a journey that would lead her to create SPANX, a billion-dollar company that revolutionized the undergarment industry. In March 2012, Sara was named the world's youngest self-made female billionaire by *Forbes* magazine and one of *Time*'s 100 Most Influential People.

Sara's story of aligned, inspired action began long before that frustrating day going door-to-door. At sixteen, following a series of personal tragedies, her father handed her a set of Dr. Wayne Dyer cassette tapes titled *How to Be a No-Limit Person*. These tapes introduced Sara to the concepts of visualization, the Law of Attraction, and the power of mindset. This early lesson on mindset laid the foundation for everything that followed. Years later, when Sara found herself in that "wrong movie" moment, she had the tools to change her reality. She didn't just complain or give up—she took aligned, inspired action.

Sara didn't force an idea or frantically try to invent something for two years after writing her intention. Instead, she remained open and receptive, trusting that the right idea would come. She waited patiently, asking herself about every opportunity that crossed her path, saying: "Are you my idea? Maybe you are the idea that I have asked for." Then, one evening, inspiration struck as Sara was getting ready for a party. She realized she didn't have the right undergarment to provide a smooth look under white pants. Armed with scissors and sheer genius, she cut the feet off her control-top pantyhose—and the SPANX revolution began!

Now, you might be thinking, "Two years? That's a long time to wait!" But Sara wasn't just sitting around twiddling her thumbs during those years. She was actively cocreating with the Universe. She kept her day job, stayed open to opportunities, and trusted the process. And look at the result: a billion-dollar company that's changed millions of lives.

Your journey might take less than two years. It might take more. The key is to understand that aligned, inspired action isn't about timelines; it's about trust, openness, and consistent movement in the direction of your dreams. When the inspiration for SPANX finally hit, Sara was ready. But even then, she didn't rush. She kept her day job, worked on her idea in the evenings, drove to North Carolina to pitch to manufacturers in person, and wrote her own patent application to save money. Each step aligned with her vision and intuition. She wasn't grinding herself down. She was following the breadcrumbs of inspiration, taking risks when it felt right, and moving consistently toward her goal.

This is what I love to call "aligned, inspired action." It's not about manufacturing your desires through sheer force of will. It's not about working yourself to the bone or sacrificing everything for your goals. That's forced action, and sure, it can get results, but at what cost?

Aligned, inspired action is different. It's about setting clear intentions, staying open to guidance, and taking consistent, inspired steps toward your vision. It's about cocreating with the Universe, not fighting against it.

Many people get stuck here. They've done the inner work we've discussed in previous chapters—the meditation, the visualizations, the gratitude practices—but they're waiting for some big, clear sign before they take action. Here's the truth: sometimes, we must make the first move. We must step out onto the dance floor before the Universe can meet us there. This chapter explores how to take aligned, inspired action. We'll examine how to recognize the difference between forced and inspired action. We'll also discuss what to do when the path isn't crystal clear and how to keep moving forward even when you're not seeing immediate results.

Whether you're manifesting love, abundance, a new career, or any other desire, the principles of aligned, inspired action apply. It's about finding that sweet spot where your actions are in harmony with your vision, your intuition, and the subtle guidance of the Universe. Sara Blakely went from frustrated fax machine salesperson to billionaire entrepreneur through aligned, inspired action. She didn't just dream about change; she took inspired steps to make it happen. Now it's your turn. Are you ready to stop wanting and start cocreating?

Forced Action vs. Aligned, Inspired Action

Most of us have been conditioned to believe in forced action our whole lives. It's the "hustle culture" mentality—the idea that success comes only through relentless work, long hours, and sacrificing everything else. It's the world of all-nighters, eighty-hour workweeks, and grinding yourself down in pursuit of your goals. I vividly remember my days as a real estate agent, constantly pushing myself to make more sales, work longer hours, and always chase the next big deal. On paper, I was successful, but in reality, I was exhausted, stressed, and pretty miserable. That's the insidious nature of forced action—it might yield results, but it often leaves you feeling drained and unfulfilled.

Forced action is like trying to control every aspect of your manifestation journey. It's a tempting trap, especially when you're eager to see immediate signs or results. When frustration sets in, it's natural to want to force outcomes, to make things happen through sheer will. But this approach is akin to a gardener trying to force a seed to bloom before its time. It's exhausting, stressful, and often counterproductive.

Why does forced action feel so hard? Because it goes against the natural flow of energy. It's like swimming upstream, constantly battling against the current. You might make progress but at what cost to your energy and well-being? It's a path that often leads to burnout and disillusionment.

In contrast, aligned action feels fundamentally different. It's about flowing with the current, not against it. It's trusting in the process and remaining open to the unfolding possibilities. Aligned action is smooth, it's energizing, and it feels right, even when it involves stepping out of your comfort zone. It's about being in tune with your intuition and the signs the Universe is sending you.

Let me share a personal example that illustrates the power of aligned, inspired action: Three months before we moved to Cornwall, I received an unexpected phone call from a storage unit manager. I had almost forgotten that I'd put our name on a waiting list six months earlier. Out of the blue, she called to say a unit was available. Now, here's where aligned action differs from forced action. At this point, we had no concrete plans to move. We didn't have a house in Cornwall, nor did we have a clear timeline for relocating. Logically, it might have made sense to decline the offer. After all, why pay for storage in Cornwall when we didn't know when we'd move?

But I saw this call as a sign, a nudge from the Universe. Instead of letting fear or logic hold me back, I took aligned, inspired action. We decided to move the contents of our house into this storage unit in Cornwall, even though we were still living four hours away at Corisande's parents' house.

People thought we were crazy. "Why are you moving your belongings when you haven't even found a place to live?" they asked. But here's the thing: Most people would wait (staying in a state of lack) and only make the move when everything was "perfect." But that's like being grateful only after something manifests. As you've learned, the key is to be grateful and act as if your desire has already manifested.

By moving our belongings to Cornwall, we were energetically aligning ourselves with our future reality before it had fully materialized. It was a powerful statement to the Universe: "We're committed to this move. We're already there in spirit." This is what aligned, inspired action looks like. It's not about pushing against the current, but flowing with it. It's taking action that feels right, that energizes you rather than depletes you. It's listening to your intuition, following the signs, and moving in harmony with the Universe.

Here's where people often get confused: aligned, inspired action doesn't mean sitting back and waiting for the Universe to do all the work. Remember Sara Blakely's story? She didn't just visualize SPANX into existence. She acted—but it was inspired action, aligned with her vision and values.

Understanding the difference between forced action and aligned, inspired action is crucial because it fundamentally changes how you approach your manifestation journey. To help illustrate this contrast, I've created a table that breaks down the key indicators of each approach. Take a moment to review this table. It provides a clear visual representation of how these two types of action differ across various criteria.

Criteria	Forced Action	Aligned, Inspired Action
Energy	Often leaves you feeling drained and burned out	Leaves you feeling energized and fulfilled
Intuition	Often goes against your gut feeling	Feels right, even if it's scary
Flow	Feels like pushing a boulder uphill	Has a sense of flow and ease, even when it's hard work
Results	Might bring short-term gains, often at a high personal cost	Tends to bring results that feel right and sustainable
Motivation	Often driven by fear or lack	Comes from a place of passion and purpose
Future focus	Often neglects long-term consequences	Considers the impact on your future self and aligns with your overall vision
Openness to signs	Plows ahead, regardless of external cues	Stays open to signs and synchronicities, adjusting course as needed

As you can see from the table, aligned, inspired action consistently leads to more positive, sustainable outcomes. It's not just about what you do, but also how you feel while doing it. This shift in perspective is transformative. Instead of asking yourself, "What do I need to force myself to do in order to get what I want?" you'll start asking, "What inspired actions can I take that align with my vision?" This simple change in questioning can lead to dramatically different results.

I encourage you to reflect on your own experiences. Think about a time when you took forced action toward a goal. How did it feel in your body? What was your energy like? What were the short-term and long-term results? Now, contrast that with a time when you took aligned, inspired action. What was different about the experience? How did it feel? What kinds of results did it yield?

By consciously choosing aligned, inspired action over forced action, you're not just changing your approach to manifestation, you're also transforming your entire relationship with the process of creating your reality. You're moving from a place of struggle and resistance to one of flow and cocreation with the Universe.

How to Take Action When Signs Are Scarce

You're doing everything by the book—meditating, defining clear goals, breaking them into smaller steps, and asking for signs—yet nothing seems to be happening. What should you do when the Universe seems silent?

This common predicament can feel frustrating, especially

when you're following all the prescribed steps to manifestation. At these moments, when progress stalls and signs are nowhere to be seen, manifestation's true challenge presents itself. This isn't the time to doubt the process; it's the time to double down and actively cocreate with the Universe.

Let me share a story that illustrates this principle in action: Sam, a client of mine, worked for a corporate tech company specializing in productivity. He had the flexibility to work from home but felt a persistent tug to strike out on his own. Despite this flexibility, he found himself stuck, operating in a mindset of lack. He was physically free to work from anywhere, yet he confined himself to his home office—a space that, although comfortable, did nothing to inspire or invigorate his entrepreneurial spirit. Sam's dream was to launch his own business as a productivity coach, helping business owners streamline their processes. He envisioned a vibrant work environment, surrounded by the buzz of fellow entrepreneurs and freelancers, in a lively coffee shop setting. However, he hesitated, waiting for a sign or the perfect moment to leave his job and dive into this new venture.

When Sam expressed frustration over the lack of signs, I challenged him to rethink his strategy. "Why wait for the perfect moment or a sign from the Universe when you could create that moment yourself?" I asked. "Why not start embodying your future self now, despite the uncertainties?"

Motivated by this shift in perspective, Sam began to spend his mornings in local coffee shops. This small change in routine didn't just alter his surroundings; it also transformed his mindset. He was no longer a hopeful entrepreneur waiting for a break; he became an active participant in the scene he wanted to join. This aligned action—simply working from a coffee shop—put him in the path of potential clients and collaborators.

One morning, a casual conversation with a fellow café-goer turned into a business opportunity. This individual became Sam's first client, catalyzing a chain of referrals that launched his dream business into reality. Sam had stopped waiting for signs and had started creating them by aligning his actions with his aspirations.

This example underscores a powerful lesson in manifestation: sometimes the most aligned action is to live out the reality you aspire to, even before it fully materializes. Don't wait for signs; become the sign. Act as if your goals have already been achieved, and let your daily actions reflect that reality. This principle applies to any area of life where you want to manifest change. For example:

1. If you're manifesting love: What would you be doing if you were already in that loving relationship? How could you get yourself out there more? Could you join social groups or classes that align with your interests?

2. If you're manifesting a new career: What skills would your future self have? Could you start taking courses or attending industry events now?

3. If you're manifesting better health: What habits would your healthiest self have? Could you start incorporating some of those habits into your routine now?

4. If you're manifesting financial abundance: How would your future wealthy self manage money?

Could you start adopting some of those practices now, even on a smaller scale?

Remember, manifestation isn't just about attracting things to you. It's about becoming the person who naturally attracts those things. Taking the right action, even without clear signs, sends a powerful message to the Universe.

This active participation changes everything. You're not just waiting for the Universe to respond but actively cocreating with it. By aligning your actions with your vision, you're making it easier for that field of intelligence to collapse opportunities into fruition.

This is the essence of aligned, inspired action—not forcing outcomes, but flowing with the energy of your future self and trusting in the cocreative process with the Universe. It's about bridging the gap between your current reality and your desired future by embodying that future now.

So the next time you feel stuck, or signs seem scarce, ask yourself: "What would my future self do in this situation?" Then, take that action. Be bold, be proactive, and most importantly, be the living embodiment of the reality you wish to create. The Universe responds not just to your thoughts and feelings, but to your actions as well. Make those actions count.

Discerning Intuition from Fear

Now that you've learned to recognize signs from the Universe, the next crucial step is knowing when and how to act on them.

This is where many people stumble in their manifestation journey. An opportunity presents itself—one that seems to align perfectly with your vision—but how do you know if it's truly the right move?

Think back to a time when a sign or an opportunity suddenly appeared, perfectly aligned with your vision. Remember that initial surge of excitement? But then, almost immediately, something didn't feel quite right. That knot in your stomach, that hesitation—we've all felt it. It's that moment when your body seems to know something your mind hasn't caught up with yet. This is the critical juncture where aligned, inspired action begins. The key is learning to differentiate between your intuition guiding you toward the right path and fear holding you back from necessary growth.

A few years ago I faced this exact scenario. I received my first opportunity to speak in front of a crowd of about fifty people in Glastonbury, England. This opportunity was very much in alignment with my vision, a clear sign from the Universe. But when it came, I felt this heavy, dooming feeling saying, "No, you shouldn't do this."

I had to ask myself: "Is this my intuition warning me away from a misaligned opportunity? Or is it simply fear, trying to keep me safely within the confines of my comfort zone because I've never spoken in front of such a large crowd before?"

This experience taught me a valuable lesson about taking aligned action in response to signs. Here's what I've learned: When a sign appears or an opportunity presents itself, it's crucial to slow down that analytical mind that's constantly questioning and analyzing. Our logical brain, while incredibly useful, can sometimes drown out the subtler signals of our intuition. To quiet this mental chatter and discern whether to take action, here's what I do:

1. Find a quiet space and close your eyes.
2. Take a few deep breaths to slow down your mind and become present in your body.
3. Visualize the scenario in question (in my case, giving the talk in Glastonbury).
4. Ask yourself: "Does taking action on this sign or opportunity make me feel light, excited, and expansive? Or does it make me feel heavy and contracted?"
5. Pay close attention to the sensations in your body.
6. Journal what you experience.

Through consistent practice of this technique, I've come to realize that knowing when to take aligned action primarily manifests as a feeling. It's that sixth sense, that gut feeling we often talk about but rarely take the time to truly listen to.

Here's the crucial distinction I've discovered: When it's right to take action, you might feel a sense of lightness, a bubbling excitement, or an energetic buzz around you, even if it's also a bit scary. Fear, on the other hand, feels heavy, contracted, and dense. It stops us in our tracks and makes us want to retreat from action. You might feel a heaviness, especially around your throat, or a sense of gloom settling over you.

When I went through this process before my Glastonbury speaking opportunity, I could almost see myself with wings, feeling an energy and lightness around the idea of giving the talk. This allowed me to discern that my initial hesitation was just fear trying to hold me back because it was afraid of the unknown. It wasn't my intuition warning me away from a misaligned opportunity. This clarity gave me the confidence to take aligned action and say yes to the opportunity.

Here's the crucial insight to remember: When a sign appears or an opportunity knocks, it's natural to feel a mix of excitement and terror. Fear might churn in your stomach, trying to keep you safely within your comfort zone. But here's where discernment becomes vital. If you pause, breathe, and tune in, you might sense an underlying current of expansion beneath that fear. That expansive feeling is your intuition whispering, "Take the leap. This is your path." The fear? It's just your old self, desperately trying to maintain the status quo.

This process of distinguishing between intuition and fear is the cornerstone of aligned, inspired action. It's about recognizing that growth often requires us to stretch beyond our current boundaries. Yes, it might feel risky to your ingrained patterns and beliefs. It might make your heart race and your palms sweat. But that doesn't mean it's wrong. In fact, that exhilarating feeling of extending beyond your current self, while remaining true to your vision, is often the breeding ground for profound transformation.

As you consistently practice this discernment, you'll refine your inner compass. You'll become adept at detecting the subtle nuances between intuitive nudges urging you forward and fear-based resistance holding you back. This skill, sharpened through experience, will evolve into your most reliable guide in navigating this path. It will empower you to respond to the Universe's signs with confidence and clarity, knowing that you're not just reacting, but consciously cocreating your reality.

PRACTICE:

Taking Aligned, Inspired Action

This practice is designed to help you not only interpret the Universe's signals but also translate them into purposeful actions that are aligned with your intentions.

Step 1: Sign Review and Decoding

- Spend a few moments reflecting on recent signs or synchronicities.
- List these signs in your journal.
- Analyze each sign, asking:
  - What might this sign be indicating about my path?
  - How does this connect to my goals or vision?
  - What actions could this sign be suggesting?
- Trust your intuition as you document your thoughts.

Step 2: Intuitive Check-In

- In a quiet place, center yourself with deep breaths.
- Focus on your main intention.
- In your journal, explore: "What inspired action feels aligned for today?"
- Let insights emerge naturally as you ponder this question.

Step 3: Action Brainstorm

Considering your signs and intuitive insights, jot down five to ten possible actions toward your goal. These actions could range from small to significant, such as buying a book, enrolling in a course, hiring a coach, joining a yoga class, starting swimming, or engaging in any activity that repeatedly surfaces despite your initial reservations. Think intuitively about what's been coming up but you've been dismissing. This simple step could mark the beginning of your manifestation journey. Manifestations often evolve gradually, not instantaneously. They're a process.

Step 4: Alignment Check

- Review your list of potential actions.
- Evaluate each by asking: "Does this feel energizing and aligned with my vision?"
- Notice your physical reactions—do you feel expansive or constricted?
- Circle the actions that feel most uplifting and in tune with your vision.

Step 5: Commit and Act

- Choose at least one aligned action from your highlighted list.
- Commit to taking this step within the next twenty-four hours.
- Note the specifics of when and how you'll act.
- Follow through, focusing on the sense of alignment it brings.

Step 6: Reflect and Build Momentum

- After taking action, reflect in your journal:
  - What were the emotions experienced during this step?
  - How did this action advance you toward your goal?
  - What new insights or ideas emerged?
- Decide on your next inspired action based on these reflections.

Weekly Reflection

Make it a habit to revisit this exercise at least once a week, always asking yourself, "How can I take aligned, inspired action today?" Review the signs you've decoded, set intentions for the week ahead, and allow inspired actions to flow naturally.

Remember, the key is not to wait passively for the perfect moment. Act when it feels right, even if it's challenging to distinguish between intuition and fear. Trust the process, knowing that the Universe supports your journey. If an action doesn't pan out as expected, view it not as a setback, but as guidance redirecting you toward a better path. Rejection is often protection in disguise.

Each week, aim to move the needle closer to your vision, no matter how small the step. Stay aware of signs and synchronicities, constantly reflecting and readying yourself for further action. Avoid paralysis by analysis—sometimes the best approach is just taking that next step.

By consistently bridging the gap between signs and actions, you're actively participating in cocreation with the Universe. Regularly review your signs, reconnect with your vision, and courageously take those steps toward your dreams. Remember, your future self isn't just waiting passively; it's actively guiding you toward each aligned action you take.

Embrace this practice as a dynamic, evolving process. As you grow and your vision evolves, so, too, will your aligned, inspired actions. Stay open, stay curious, and most importantly, stay in motion. The Universe rewards action, especially when it's aligned with your deepest truths and highest aspirations.

The Secret to Lasting Success with Conscious Manifestation

There's an ancient wisdom teaching known as the *butterfly effect*, which suggests that the gentle flap of a butterfly's wings can set off a chain of events leading to a hurricane on the other side of the world. As you turn these final pages, remember that you're not just finishing a book; you're initiating an enormous effect. You create that gentle flap each day as you show up, commit to your practices, and embrace small changes. And gradually, step-by-step, day by day, these small actions will have a profound impact on your life.

Think back to when you first picked up this book. Perhaps you were driven by a deep, intense desire that felt like a physical ache. You may have approached manifestation with a dose of skepticism. Wherever you started, know this: you are not the person you were when you began this journey.

You've learned that manifestation isn't about desperately

wanting or endlessly wishing. It's about being. It's about aligning your energy with the frequency of your desires, stepping into the version of yourself that already possesses what you seek. You've discovered that the power to shape your reality has always been within you, simply waiting to be activated.

The real secret, the true essence of manifestation, lies in these small steps, these thousands of tiny adjustments to your vibrational frequency. This is the heart of moving beyond wanting—it's not about one giant leap, but the consistent, small steps you take daily.

These shifts might seem insignificant in the beginning, often washed away by the weight of old habits and beliefs. One session of gratitude won't instantly manifest your desires. A single positive thought or affirmation is unlikely to deliver a noticeable difference. But don't be discouraged—this is where the magic begins. Each practice tunes you in, compounds, and grows. Eventually, if you stick with it, you'll hit a tipping point. Suddenly, staying in alignment feels easier. The weight of your new vibration works for you, not against you.

Remember, this journey will have its challenges. Life is full of obstacles, triggers, setbacks, and moments of doubt. That's the game; the fun of being human. I, too, experience these regularly. The key is not to avoid these moments but to improve your recovery time. Maintain the observer's seat. Practice awareness. Catch the triggers. Notice your limiting thoughts. Sense the heavy emotions that pull you out of alignment. With practice, you'll bounce back from setbacks more quickly, moving from days to hours to mere minutes.

Your emotional state is your compass on this journey, your

point of reference for attraction. Use the emotional resonance scale we discussed. Check in with yourself regularly. Are you vibrating at the frequency of your desires, or have you slipped into lack?

So where do you go from here? The answer is simple: Forward. Always forward. Use the tools you've learned. Practice self-observation. Catch yourself, pick yourself up. Defend your energy. Get clear. Rehearse in meditation. Write, cry, laugh, and high-five yourself. Learn, grow, and expand. Feel it. Be thankful ahead of the event. Affirm it. Let go, trust, stay open, spot the signs, and take action. Always take action. Feel the fear and lean in. Follow the steps. Take the lead. Make the move. Show up daily and do the work. Commit to this practice with unwavering dedication.

To support you on this journey, I invite you to join the thousands of readers worldwide who receive my weekly manifestation newsletter. This isn't just another email in your inbox; it's a lifeline of continued guidance, inspiration, and powerful techniques delivered straight to you. Sign up now at mattcooke.me, and let's keep this momentum going.

My manifestation journey continues alongside yours. While writing this book, I manifested the purchase of our dream house in Cornwall and the beautiful journey of becoming parents with the arrival of our son, Humphrey. These desires were my "want" at the start, but I moved beyond them and watched them unfold, chapter by chapter. Coincidentally, these manifestations have become the most significant manifestations of my life and have only deepened my conviction beyond what I thought was possible. And I promise you, this is just the beginning. New inspirations and insights are constantly flowing, and I'm committed to sharing them with you.

I'm so grateful and blessed that you've read this book because I know the information here will transform your life and positively impact countless others. Thank you, thank you, thank you.

As you close this book and step back into your life, carry this truth with you: you are the creator of your reality. You always have been. You have the power to manifest your dreams, not from a place of desperate wanting, but from a place of being.

Remember, you're always in a state of manifestation, consciously or unconsciously. But now, with this book, you hold the keys to conscious creation.

Pass along this book, share these teachings, and gift copies to friends. Let's spread this message globally: you manifest what you are, not what you want. Be the future you desire, and watch it unfold.

So go forth. Create. Manifest. Live the life you've always envisioned. Whenever you need a reminder of your power, or whenever you need to realign, this book will be here. It will always be with you.

Thank you for allowing me to be part of your journey. It's time for you to write the next chapter of your life. Make it magnificent.

You've got this.

Trust me.

Acknowledgments

This book would not exist without so many incredible souls, and I must start with my wife, Corisande, my best friend, soulmate, and absolute everything—you've believed in me from the start, taken every leap of faith with me, and helped create this life we once only dreamed of. From the quiet evenings when I wrestled with ideas to the late nights when you held our newborn son while I wrote, your trust in this journey, even when the path wasn't clear, made everything possible. None of this would exist without you.

To my son, Humphrey, my peaceful warrior, who arrived at the perfect moment as this book neared completion—you've taught me a deeper level of love and presence that I never knew existed. You are our greatest manifestation, and everything I do now is to show you that you can be and create whatever you want in life.

To my late mother, Julie—thank you for sparking both this

journey and my spiritual awakening. Through our connection, you showed me a world beyond the physical, one filled with more magic than I ever imagined possible. I know you're behind the scenes, guiding and supporting in ways I'm still discovering. Your spirit lives on in these pages.

To my brilliant mother-in-law, Georgina, who is more than just my first reader—you're a pillar of support in every area of my life. Your kindness, selflessness, and constant encouragement have made this book, and life itself, infinitely richer. Thank you for always being ready to help, for your incredible patience, and for your unwavering belief in me.

To my father, Martyn, who taught me the power of the longer game in life—your straightforward approach showed me that true success comes not from rushing or forcing outcomes, but from patience, persistence, and trust in the process.

To my father-in-law, Alan, whose deep wisdom and unique perspective have illuminated my path—your presence in my life is no coincidence. You've helped me see beyond the obvious and discover deeper truths. Thank you for showing me how to look beneath the surface of everything.

To my clients—each one of you has added layers to my understanding of manifestation. Your trust in me and your incredible stories have shaped this book in ways you'll never know. I am beyond grateful for your willingness to share your journeys with me.

To David, my friend and mentor, who saw the potential in these teachings from day one—your guidance, wisdom, and belief helped turn my dream into reality. I will be forever grateful.

To my agent, Steve, whose alignment with this project proved that the Universe brings us precisely who we need—your experience and genuine enthusiasm have made this journey both smoother and more meaningful.

To my dear friend Russell, whose deep conversations during our corporate days first awakened me to a different way of seeing life—those early discussions planted seeds that would grow into this work.

To my editor, Batya, whose meticulous attention to every detail helped unveil the book's truest form—your gift for seeing both the forest and the trees, questioning each word choice while strengthening the broader teachings, transformed this manuscript into something far beyond my initial vision. You knew exactly when to simplify and when to push deeper, always ensuring the message remained clear and authentic. Thank you for helping these teachings reach their full potential while keeping my voice intact.

To the entire Tarcher and Penguin Random House team— thank you for believing in this project and bringing it to life. From the design to the production, your expertise and dedication have made this vision a reality I am deeply proud of. Your collective brilliance has given these teachings a home that will reach readers worldwide.

To my soul family—all those I've connected with on this journey, whether briefly or profoundly—your stories, breakthroughs, and trust prove daily that manifestation is a collective journey. When we move beyond wanting together, we create ripples of transformation.

To you, the reader—thank you for walking this path with me. The power to create has always been yours; now you know how to use it. Thank you for giving your precious time to my story. Now it's your turn to create.

Finally, to the divine intelligence that flows through all things—thank you for reminding me that creation is not about doing or wanting, but about aligning with what already is. You've guided every word, every teaching, and every breakthrough that made this book possible.

Notes

In this section, you'll find a list of references, resources, and citations for each chapter in this book. My hope is that the information provided here will guide you further into the concepts discussed throughout. I've done my best to ensure accuracy in attributing ideas, stories, and scientific research to their rightful sources. However, as research, science, and understanding evolve, updates may be needed or minor errors might be discovered. If you believe any information needs correcting or clarification, please email me at matt@mattcooke.me so I can investigate it.

CHAPTER 1: THE FOUNDATIONS OF MANIFESTATION

6 *The Science of Getting Rich* by Wallace D. Wattles: Wattles discusses the practical application of thought and its power to manifest reality in his book, which can provide a historical viewpoint on the Law of Attraction as utilized in the early twentieth century. Wallace D. Wattles, *The Science of Getting Rich* (Elizabeth Towne Co., 1910).

6 *Think and Grow Rich*, published in 1937 by Napoleon Hill: Hill's work, which synthesizes the success principles of more than five hundred wealthy men, illustrates the practical application of belief and thought in achieving personal success, reinforcing the historical context of these ideas. Napoleon Hill, *Think and Grow Rich* (The Ralston Society, 1937).

6 the actor Jim Carrey: Carrey shared a powerful story about how he used visualization techniques to achieve his acting career goals during an interview with Oprah Winfrey. He described writing himself a check for ten million dollars for "acting services rendered" and dating it for Thanksgiving 1995, which later materialized when he received a similar amount for his role in *Dumb and Dumber*. "Oprah—Jim Carrey—Visualization Empowerment," July 22, 2013, video, https://www.youtube.com/watch?v=RwTS0uh2faE.

8 by age thirty-five, about 95 percent of our identity is composed of deeply ingrained patterns: Dr. Joe Dispenza examines the profound impact that habitual behaviors and subconscious programming have on our identity by the time most individuals reach their midthirties. He explains, "By the time you're in your mid-30s, you're a set of memorized behaviors, emotional reactions, unconscious habits, hardwired attitudes, beliefs, and perceptions that function like a computer program." Dr. Joe Dispenza, *Breaking the Habit of Being Yourself: How to Lose Your Mind and Create a New One* (Hay House, 2012).

11 our physical world is composed of energy: Ethan Siegel, "You Are Not Mostly Empty Space," *Forbes*, April 16, 2020, https://www.forbes.com/sites/startswithabang/2020/04/16/you-are-not-mostly-empty-space/?sh=765dbbe82c2b.

12 atoms are more than 99.9 percent empty space: Trevor English, "Due to the Space inside Atoms, You Are Mostly Made up of Empty Space," *Interesting Engineering*, February 28, 2020, https://interestingengineering.com/science/due-to-the-space-inside-atoms-you-are-mostly-made-up-of-empty-space#.

13 fluidlike substance known as quantum fields: "Quantum Fields: The
Real Building Blocks of the Universe—with David Tong," February 15,
2017, video, https://youtu.be/zNVQfWC_evg?si=bTmQ2p4Zwi
NiN7ET.

21 One of these experiments, the double-slit experiment: "Double
Slit Experiment Explained! by Jim Al-Khalili," February 1, 2013,
video, https://www.youtube.com/watch?v=A9tKncAdlHQ.

CHAPTER 2: FROM WANTING TO BEING

30 The dictionary defines *want* as: "want," Merriam-Webster.com, accessed August 31, 2024, https://www.merriam-webster.com/dictio
nary/want.

35 The story of Ali Hafed: Russell H. Conwell, "Acres of Diamonds,"
Project Gutenberg, 2008, https://www.gutenberg.org/files/368
/368-h/368-h.htm.

37 The quantum field, that invisible sea of energy: For a comprehensive explanation of the quantum field theory, see Frank Wilczek,
The Lightness of Being: Mass, Ether, and the Unification of Forces (Basic Books, 2008). In it, Wilczek, a Nobel laureate in physics, provides
an accessible overview of quantum field theory and its implications
for our understanding of the universe.

37 *Indiana Jones and the Last Crusade*: Steven Spielberg, dir., *Indiana Jones and the Last Crusade* (Paramount Pictures, 1989). The invisible bridge scene occurs at approximately one hour, fifty-four
minutes into the film. This scene metaphorically represents the
concept of faith and trust in the unseen, which is a central theme
in manifestation practices.

CHAPTER 3: SELF-OBSERVATION

47 Psychologists Daniel Simons and Christopher Chabris, while working at Harvard University, conducted an experiment: Daniel J.

Simons and Christopher F. Chabris, "Gorillas in Our Midst: Sustained Inattentional Blindness for Dynamic Events," *Perception* 28, no. 9 (1999): 1059–1074, https://doi.org/10.1068/p281059.

50 **You can take the blue pill:** This analogy is a reference to the 1999 film *The Matrix*, directed by the Wachowsks. In the film, taking the blue pill allows one to remain in blissful ignorance, while taking the red pill leads to harsh truth and reality.

55 **The researchers found that many participants struggled to sit alone with their thoughts:** Timothy D. Wilson et al., "Just Think: The Challenges of the Disengaged Mind," *Science* 345, no. 6192 (July 4, 2014): 75–77, https://doi.org/10.1126/science.1250830.

57 **this awareness of your thoughts is known as *metacognition*:** "Metacognitive awareness is the ability to decenter from thoughts and emotions, viewing them as passing mental events rather than identifying with them or believing thoughts to be accurate representations of reality." Michaela C. Pascoe et al., "Psychobiological Mechanisms Underlying the Mood Benefits of Meditation: A Narrative Review," *Comprehensive Psychoneuroendocrinology* 6 (May 2021): section 3.1.5, https://doi.org/10.1016/j.cpnec.2021.100037.

64 **"drink his food and chew his water":** Jay Shetty, *Think Like a Monk: Train Your Mind for Peace and Purpose Every Day* (Simon & Schuster, 2020), 153.

70 **the power of "habit stacking":** James Clear, *Atomic Habits: An Easy & Proven Way to Build Good Habits & Break Bad Ones* (Avery, 2018), 74–75.

CHAPTER 4: YOUR VISION

73 **the first Black woman in space:** Vickie Lindsey, "She Had a Dream: Mae C. Jemison, First African American Woman in Space," Smithsonian National Air and Space Museum, September 12, 2010,

https://airandspace.si.edu/stories/editorial/she-had-dream-mae-c
-jemison-first-african-american-woman-space.

73 **"Never limit yourself because of others' limited imagination":**
Mae C. Jemison, quoted in "Mae C. Jemison," Biography.com, accessed February 28, 2025, https://www.biography.com/scientists
/mae-c-jemison.

78 **What sets apart the Be-Do-Have approach:** Stephen R. Covey, *The
7 Habits of Highly Effective People* (Free Press, 1989). In his book,
Covey introduces the Be-Do-Have paradigm as a framework for
personal development and achieving one's goals.

87 **reticular activating system (RAS):** Dhanalakshmi Harikrishnan
and Sharon Linde, "Reticular Activating System | Definition &
Function," Study.com, November 21, 2023, https://study.com/acad
emy/lesson/reticular-activating-system-definition-function.html.

CHAPTER 5: BELIEVE

96 **Princeton Engineering Anomalies Research (PEAR) program:**
Robert G. Jahn and Brenda J. Dunne delve into the interplay between consciousness and physical reality, discussing the extensive research conducted under the PEAR program at Princeton
University. For an in-depth exploration of this research and its
implications, see Jahn and Dunne, *Margins of Reality: The Role of
Consciousness in the Physical World* (Princeton University Press,
1987; reprinted by ICRL Press, 2009).

98 **French researcher René Peoc'h conducted an extraordinary experiment:** As cited in Joe Dispenza, *Becoming Supernatural: How
Common People Are Doing the Uncommon* (Hay House, 2017), 73–74.

104 **"Give me a child until he is seven, and I will show you the man":**
This quote is often attributed to Aristotle, but its exact origin is
debated. For a scientific perspective on early childhood development, see National Research Council and Institute of Medicine,

From Neurons to Neighborhoods: The Science of Early Childhood Development (National Academy Press, 2000).

112 **In a pioneering study, Dr. Phillippa Lally:** Phillippa Lally, et al., "How Are Habits Formed: Modelling Habit Formation in the Real World," *European Journal of Social Psychology* 40, no. 6 (2009), 998–1009, https://doi.org/10.1002/ejsp.674.

CHAPTER 6: REHEARSE

119 **a fascinating study done by researchers at the Cleveland Clinic Foundation:** Vinoth K. Ranganathan, et al., "From Mental Power to Muscle Power—Gaining Strength by Using the Mind," *Neuropsychologia* 42, no. 7 (2004), 944–956, https://doi.org/10.1016/j.neuro psychologia.2003.11.018.

120 **Michael Phelps, the most decorated Olympian of all time:** "Michael Phelps," Olympics.com, https://olympics.com/en/athletes/michael-phelps-ii.

120 **Bob Bowman, recognized the importance of mental preparation:** Bowman discusses providing Michael Phelps's mother with a book on progressive relaxation in an interview. "Visualization Used by Michael Phelps," November 2, 2020, video, https://www.youtube.com/watch?v=3-mm90LFPqU.

121 **In a YouTube interview, he explained how he also prepared his mind:** Michael Phelps discusses his visualization techniques in an interview with ProSwimwear: "Michael Phelps—The Journey—Ep 5—Visualization," August 20, 2018, video, https://www.youtube.com/watch?v=p-mZhvxeK_k.

122 **During the two-hundred-meter butterfly final at the 2008 Olympics:** Karen Crouse, "Phelps's Epic Journey Ends in Fitting Style," *The New York Times*, August 17, 2008, https://www.nytimes.com/2008/08/17/sports/olympics/17swim.html.

123 a phenomenon called *neuroplasticity*: Norman Doidge, *The Brain That Changes Itself: Stories of Personal Triumph from the Frontiers of Brain Science* (Penguin Books, 2007). This book provides an accessible introduction to neuroplasticity and its implications for personal change.

124 "Neurons that fire together, wire together": This phrase is attributed to neuropsychologist Donald Hebb. For more information, see D. O. Hebb, *The Organization of Behavior: A Neuropsychological Theory* (Wiley, 1949).

125 your brain starts to treat your visualized future as a real: For scientific research on this concept, see Stephen M. Kosslyn, et al., *The Case for Mental Imagery* (Oxford University Press, 2006). This book reviews extensive research on how mental imagery affects brain function.

132 music has the ability to evoke emotions and transport us to different mental states: For scientific research on how music affects our emotions and mental states, see Stefan Koelsch, "Brain Correlates of Music-Evoked Emotions," *Nature Reviews Neuroscience* 15 (2014), 170–180, https://doi.org/10.1038/nrn3666.

CHAPTER 7: FEEL IT TILL YOU MAKE IT

140 It's what psychologists call "cognitive dissonance": For more on this psychological concept, see Leon Festinger, *A Theory of Cognitive Dissonance* (Stanford University Press, 1957).

141 one of the UK's top holiday destinations: Cornwall's appeal as a top UK holiday destination is well documented. According to *The Guardian*, Cornwall attracts about five million tourists each year, significantly impacting the local community and housing market. For more details, see Natasha Carthew, "Welcome to Cornwall! Please Don't Ruin It for Us Local People," *The Guardian*, May 29,

2023, https://www.theguardian.com/commentisfree/2023/may/29
/welcome-to-cornwall-please-dont-ruin-it-for-us-local-people.

148 **Dr. David Hawkins, a psychiatrist and consciousness researcher:**
David R. Hawkins, *Power vs. Force: The Hidden Determinants of Human Behavior* (Hay House, 2002).

150 **the revolutionary insights of Dr. Joe Dispenza:** Dr. Joe Dispenza, *Becoming Supernatural: How Common People Are Doing the Uncommon* (Hay House, 2017).

163 **Emotional Freedom Technique (EFT):** For more information on EFT and its scientific basis, see Gary Craig, *The EFT Manual* (Energy Psychology Press, 2011).

CHAPTER 8: JOURNALING

167 **"morning pages":** Julia Cameron, *The Artist's Way: A Spiritual Path to Higher Creativity* (TarcherPerigee, 2002).

CHAPTER 9: GRATITUDE

179 *The Magic* **by Rhonda Byrne:** Rhonda Byrne, *The Magic* (Atria Books, 2012).

184 **Psychologist Ellen Langer and her colleagues at Harvard conducted a fascinating study:** Ellen J. Langer, et al., "The Mindlessness of Ostensibly Thoughtful Action: The Role of 'Placebic' Information in Interpersonal Interaction," *Journal of Personality and Social Psychology* 36, no. 6 (1978): 635–642, https://doi.org/10.1037/0022-3514.36.6.635.

193 **Dave Ramsey, a renowned financial adviser, teaches a concept called the *debt snowball*:** Dave Ramsey, *The Total Money Makeover: A Proven Plan for Financial Fitness* (Thomas Nelson, 2013).

CHAPTER 10: AFFIRMATIONS

196 **French pharmacist Émile Coué:** For a detailed explanation of Coué's method and its applications, see C. Harry Brooks, *The Practice of Autosuggestion by the Method of Emile Coué* (Dodd, Mead and Company, 1922). This book is available online at Project Gutenberg, https://www.gutenberg.org/files/29339/29339-h/29339-h.htm.

197 **The results of Coué's method were remarkable:** Émile Coué, *Self Mastery Through Conscious Autosuggestion* (American Library Service, 1922).

198 **one of the most famous examples of the use of affirmations is by Muhammad Ali:** For a detailed account of Ali's use of affirmations and positive self-talk, see Thomas Hauser, *Muhammad Ali: His Life and Times* (Simon & Schuster, 1991), particularly pages 146 through 148. Hauser's biography, based on more than five hundred interviews with Ali's associates, provides comprehensive insight into Ali's mental approach to boxing and life.

201 **When you repeat these statements daily, they become paradigms:** For a scientific perspective on how our subconscious beliefs shape our reality, see Bruce Lipton, *The Biology of Belief: Unleashing the Power of Consciousness, Matter & Miracles* (Hay House, 2016). Lipton, a cell biologist, explains how our thoughts and beliefs influence our cellular biology and overall health, providing a scientific foundation for the power of affirmations and positive thinking.

208 **"If you only knew the magnificence of the three, six, and nine":** This quote is widely attributed to Nikola Tesla, but there's no definitive historical source for it. It's become part of the popular narrative around Tesla. Readers should approach it as anecdotal rather than verified.

208 **Marko Rodin believes that three, six, and nine represent a "flux field":** See Soundarya, "369: Key to the Universe!" Medium, August 27, 2023, https://soundarya369.medium.com/369-key-to-the -universe-a794a479c433.

209 **Tesla was bouncing between cheap hotels and died in room number 3327:** Mark Singer, "Tesla Slept Here," *The New Yorker*, January 7, 2008, https://www.newyorker.com/magazine/2008/01/14/tesla -slept-here.

CHAPTER 11: LET GO

217 **"Rejection is protection":** Gabrielle (Gabby) Bernstein shared this mantra on her Instagram (https://www.instagram.com/gabbyber nstein/reel/C2LXfCNxIwS/) and frequently discusses similar concepts of reframing obstacles as guidance. For a deeper exploration of this idea, see chapter 6 of her book *The Universe Has Your Back* (Hay House, 2016), where she discusses viewing obstacles and detours as divine redirection.

220 **When offered a chance to audition for *The Girl from Petrovka*, Hopkins set out to find a copy:** This remarkable coincidence is recounted in Rachel Martin, "Why Confounding Coincidences Happen Every Day," NPR, February 9, 2014, https://www.npr.org /2014/02/09/274075349/why-confounding-coincidences-happen -every-day.

221 **we perceive about 0.0035 percent of the entire electromagnetic spectrum:** According to NASA, "The electromagnetic spectrum is the range of all types of EM radiation. Radiation is energy that travels and spreads out as it goes. . . . Visible light is the only part of the EM spectrum we can see. It ranges from about 380 to 700 nanometers in wavelength. . . . The full EM spectrum is about 100 million times as wide as the visible spectrum." This means humans can see approximately 0.0035 percent of the entire electromagnetic spectrum. See "Introduction to the Electromagnetic Spectrum," NASA Science, accessed August 14, 2024, https://science.nasa.gov/ems/01_intro.

221 **that invisible 99.9965 percent of reality invisible to the human eye:** This percentage is derived from the fact that humans can only

perceive about 0.0035 percent of the electromagnetic spectrum, leaving 99.9965 percent imperceptible to the human eye.

222 **Think of the ego as your inner bodyguard:** For a comprehensive understanding of the ego in psychology, particularly from a Jungian perspective, see: C. G. Jung, *The Portable Jung*, edited by Joseph Campbell (Penguin Books, 1971). Jung's view of the ego as a complex part of the psyche that mediates between the conscious and unconscious aligns well with the concept of the ego as an "inner bodyguard" in manifestation work.

223 **This is where FEAR (false evidence appearing real):** This acronym is often attributed to various sources, but its origin is unclear. It's widely used in self-help and motivational contexts.

CHAPTER 12: SIGNS

229 *The Silva Mind Control Method*: José Silva and Philip Miele, *The Silva Mind Control Method: The Revolutionary Program by the Founder of the World's Most Famous Mind Control Course* (Pocket Books, 1977). This book outlines Silva's techniques for enhancing brain function, including methods for dream recall and receiving guidance through dreams.

241 **Greek mathematician and philosopher Pythagoras:** For a comprehensive exploration of Pythagoras's life, see Christoph Riedweg, *Pythagoras: His Life, Teaching, and Influence* (Cornell University Press, 2012). This scholarly work provides in-depth insights into Pythagoras's teachings and their lasting impact on Western thought.

241 **string theory and M-theory:** For an accessible introduction to string theory and multiple dimensions, see Brian Greene, *The Elegant Universe: Superstrings, Hidden Dimensions, and the Quest for the Ultimate Theory* (W. W. Norton & Company, 2003).

246 **the meanings of angel numbers:** The interpretations provided in this book are based on a synthesis of various sources and, most

importantly, my personal experiences and observations during years of practice. For readers interested in exploring other perspectives, see Doreen Virtue, *Angel Numbers 101: The Meaning of 111, 123, 444, and Other Number Sequences* (Hay House, 2008) and Kyle Gray, *Angel Numbers: The Message and Meaning Behind 11:11 and Other Number Sequences* (Hay House, 2019). It's important to note that interpretations of angel numbers can vary widely among different authors and practitioners. I encourage readers to use these resources, including my own interpretations, as starting points for developing their own understanding based on personal experiences and intuition.

CHAPTER 13: ALIGNED, INSPIRED ACTION

249 **Around the late 1990s, a young woman was having a particularly rough day:** Sara Blakely shares this story in an interview with ForbesWomen. "Sara Blakely on the Origin Story of Spanx: 'I Was Just a Frustrated Consumer,'" November 3, 2021, video, https://www.youtube.com/watch?v=3hCtukSt_e0.

250 **In March 2012, Sara was named:** Clare O'Connor, "How Sara Blakely of Spanx Turned $5,000 into $1 Billion," *Forbes*, March 14, 2012, https://www.forbes.com/global/2012/0326/billionaires-12 -feature-united-states-spanx-sara-blakely-american-booty.html.

250 **her father handed her a set of Dr. Wayne Dyer cassette tapes:** "Sarah Blakely: This Is the Only Reason Why Spanx Exists Today," Michael Simmons, December 6, 2020, video, https://www.youtube .com/watch?v=QE9E_ON73C0.

About the Author

Matt Cooke is a renowned manifestation coach, speaker, and thought leader who inspires a global audience with his modern approach to spirituality. After nearly a decade in real estate, he took a transformative leap to launch a successful digital marketing business before fully dedicating himself to the art and science of manifestation. Committed to helping people create their best lives and achieve their dreams, Matt shares accessible, practical advice on social media and provides guided meditations, workshops, keynotes, online courses, and coaching. He lives with his wife, Corisande, and their son, Humphrey, in Cornwall, United Kingdom.